W9-AAL-780

Everything You Need to Know to
"Talk" a Great Game

G●LF
A to Z

CHRIS BURKHART

LPGA National Education Instructor

Contemporary Books

Chicago   New York   San Francisco   Lisbon   London   Madrid   Mexico City
Milan   New Delhi   San Juan   Seoul   Singapore   Sydney   Toronto

Library of Congress Cataloging-in-Publication Data

Burkhart, Chris.
    Golf A to Z : everything you need to know to "talk" a great game / Chris Burkhart.
       p.   cm.
    ISBN 0-07-138558-4
    1. Golf—Terminology.   I. Title.

  GV961.3 .B87   2002
  796.352'03—dc21   2002019313

Contemporary Books

*A Division of The **McGraw·Hill** Companies*

Copyright © 2002 by Chris Burkhart. All rights reserved. Printed in the United States of America.
Except as permitted under the United States Copyright Act of 1976, no part of this publication may
be reproduced or distributed in any form or by any means, or stored in a database or retrieval
system, without the prior written permission of the publisher.

1 2 3 4 5 6 7 8 9 0   LBM/LBM   1 0 9 8 7 6 5 4 3 2

ISBN 0-07-138558-4

This book was set in Goudy
Printed and bound by Lake Book Manufacturing

Interior design by Laurie Young

McGraw-Hill books are available at special quantity discounts to use as premiums and sales
promotions, or for use in corporate training programs. For more information, please write to the
Director of Special Sales, Professional Publishing, McGraw-Hill, Two Penn Plaza, New York, NY
10121-2298. Or contact your local bookstore.

This book is printed on acid-free paper.

For allowing me to play any sport I wanted as a child
as long as I learned to play golf,
for helping me appreciate that golf is truly a lifelong sport,
and for supporting golf as my career,
thank you, Mom and Dad

Contents

Preface

Golf A to Z is for anyone with an interest in golf. It is informative and fun to read as it takes you from pro shop to tees, through fairways and greens and back to the clubhouse, explaining how more than 1,000 terms and phrases are commonly used; it is written in everyday language that's easy to understand. Also included is a complete index of terms, so you can easily find any term you want whenever you want it.

As I was developing the content for *Golf A to Z*, I discovered that every person—golf instructors, pro tour players, new and experienced amateur golfers, and those who might talk about golf but not necessarily play it—has a certain number of terms and phrases they use. But I have yet to meet any one person in any of these categories who knows the meaning of every term included in this book. One retired senior golfer even told me that he learned more sitting on his behind reading this book than he had learned on his feet playing the game for more than 60 years. What a compliment!

The purpose of *Golf A to Z* is to make the language of golf user-friendly. If you play the game, or watch tournaments in person or on TV, or are learning to play (or thinking about it), *Golf A to Z* will enhance your arsenal of golf terms so that you can "talk" a great game!

Pro Shop
Patter

196

Helpful Terms
to Know
Before You Play

ABOUT THE GAME OF GOLF

The game of golf is, in principle, very simple to play. You hit a ball with a club as few times as possible to get it from a designated starting point into a designated hole in the ground. Then you repeat this process for an entire series of holes until the ball has entered the last hole. Golf is truly one of the few sports that appeals equally to youth and to men and women of all ages. Golf has many unique characteristics. For example, you can play by yourself, or you can play with (or compete against) others.

Stroke

A stroke is a swing of the club in an effort to hit the ball. The object of golf is for each stroke to be as effective as possible in moving the ball toward or into the hole. Every stroke you take counts toward your score for the entire game, which is called a round.

Round of Golf

A round of golf is usually either 9 or 18 holes of play.

Goal of the Game

In most cases, the goal of the game is to have the fewest number of strokes possible at the end of a round.

Golf Course
Course

Golf is played on a golf course, defined as the whole area within which play is permitted. The term golf course is often abbreviated to course.

Hole

The term hole has two primary meanings in the game of golf, and both are used constantly. A hole of play refers to each designated area on a course from the tee to a corresponding hole on the green. All golf courses are classified according to the number of holes available for play.

A second definition of hole refers to the actual cylindrical sleeve cut into the putting green. This hole looks much like an empty soup can sunk into the ground so that the top edges are even with the putting surface.

Signature Hole

Most golf courses have a signature hole, which is not necessarily the course's most difficult hole to play but is the most memorable. Many courses use photos of their signature holes for promotional purposes.

Par

While par is defined as average in dictionaries and crossword puzzles, in golf it means excellence. When you par any hole of play, it means you have used only a predetermined number of strokes to get the ball from the tee into the hole.

Par for the Course

The goal for most competitive golfers is to be par or better for the course. This happens when someone has a total score of par or better for an entire round.

ABOUT GOLF COURSES

Regulation Course

A golf course is a regulation course only if it has par-3, par-4, and par-5 holes. All USGA-sanctioned tournaments and other official play are on regulation courses, which must be at least 9 holes but are usually 18.

The Royal and Ancient Golf Club of St. Andrews, Scotland (R & A)

The Royal and Ancient Golf Club of St. Andrews, Scotland, often abbreviated "R & A," was officially formed in 1754, many years after the game of golf became popular in Scotland. The purpose of the R & A is to preserve and enhance the integrity and rules of the game throughout the world.

The USGA
United States Golf Association

The USGA (United States Golf Association) was established in 1894. The USGA is the governing body for golf within the United States, working in concert with the R & A.

The Rules of Golf

The USGA and the R & A have authority over the game and administer its rules through the official publication *The Rules of Golf*, which is now in its 28th edition and has been translated into more than 20 languages for use throughout the world.

Summer Rules

When playing by summer rules, golfers must play the ball as it lies, which means that they must play the ball however they find it without improving its position in any way. Summer rules are always in effect unless course officials declare otherwise.

Play the Ball Down

Play the ball down is another way to say that the course is being played by summer rules. The ball may not be moved at all during play, except in accordance with *The Rules of Golf*.

Winter Rules
Preferred Lies

Since almost all golf courses are outdoors, weather is a major factor in how a course plays on any given day. Under certain conditions, course officials may declare winter rules, or preferred lies, to be in effect. Winter rules permit a golfer to move his ball on any shot (except in hazards or on greens) a specified distance to compensate for bad course conditions. Under these rules, players may also lift and clean their golf ball before placing it to take their next shot.

Roll the Ball Over

Roll the ball over is a casual way of describing how winter rules are applied. Golfers can use the head of their club—rather than hands, feet, or anything else—to move the ball to a better spot for their next shot.

Public Course

At public courses, members of the general public pay a fee to play 9 or 18 holes. There are no memberships available.

Municipal Course

Many public courses that are owned by public entities, like a city, are called municipal courses.

Daily Fee Course

A daily fee course is a public course that charges golfers a single fee to play all day, regardless of the number of rounds or holes they complete.

Private Course

Only owners, dues-paying members, and their personal guests are permitted to play at a private course. The general public is not allowed.

Semiprivate Course

A semiprivate course offers memberships but is open to the general public as well.

Resort Course

A resort course is open to the public. Typically, a resort course has a variety of recreational and service facilities in addition to the golf course, and offers hotel or motel accommodations as well. Many resort courses are well maintained and expensive to play.

Stadium Course

A stadium course is a course designed so that spectators can see as much action as possible. This type of course has grassy slopes and hillsides around many of its tees and greens, where spectators get a view similar to that provided by an outdoor football stadium but without actual stadium seats.

Country Club

In addition to a members-only golf course, a typical country club has a swimming pool, tennis courts, a clubhouse with food and beverage service and full-service dining, locker rooms, a pro shop, and a driving range.

Golf Club (the Place)

A golf club is similar to a country club in that it offers membership privileges, clubhouse facilities, and food and beverage service, but most golf clubs have no amenities other than golf.

Reciprocal Play

When a golf club hosts a tournament, club members who are not playing in the tournament are sometimes permitted to play at another private club. This transfer of playing privileges for a specific day or period is called reciprocal play.

Links Course

A links course, which can be either public or private, is so named because of its location near an ocean and undulating, sandy ground. Most true links courses are found in the British Isles, and they are the preferred sites for the British Open. Many golfers and TV commentators are fond of talking about links course design and how proximity to the coast—which usually means ever-present wind and firm turf—influences playing conditions on these courses. Play on links courses often turns into a battle between a player and the elements.

Public Links
Public links is a term that refers to any nonmembership course, which is not to be confused with a true links course.

Links
Public links is often abbreviated to simply links.

Target Golf Course
Target golf courses have a nonstandard design. Instead of continuous groomed fairways between tees and greens, a target course has landing areas—or targets—that are placed at intervals where the designer expects golfers to hit the ball. The rest of the course is natural terrain. This type of course encourages golfers to hit as accurately as possible because there is no playable alternative when targets are missed. A target course often yields a higher score than typical courses do.

Executive Course
An executive course has no par-5 holes, only par 3's and par 4's that are typically shorter than those found on a regulation course. This promotes fast play and requires less long-game skill. An executive course is ideal for cor-

porate types who like to play a quick round and then brag about their low scores.

Par-3 Course
A par-3 course is one that has designated all its holes as par-3 holes, no matter how long or difficult they are.

Pitch-and-Putt Course
A pitch-and-putt course also has only par-3 holes, but no hole of play is longer than 100 yards.

Driving Range
A traditional driving range has teeing areas, designed for full swing practice, that are covered with real grass or mats made of artificial turf. Many ranges are stand-alone operations; others are located within golf courses.

Range Balls
Double-Striper
Range balls are practice balls that a course or range rents by the bucket. Range balls aren't designed to be used on an actual golf course. Many range balls have two large stripes—and thus they have gotten the nickname double-striper.

Shag Bag
Range Picker
To retrieve balls so that they can be used repeatedly, a course or range may employ a person equipped with a handheld shag bag, which is designed so that the person

retrieving balls doesn't have to bend over. A motorized range picker, which resembles a large riding lawn mower, may be used to retrieve the balls.

Floater Ball

Some golf courses have driving ranges that contain lakes, designed so that golfers hit range balls, called floater balls, into the water. Balls float on the lake's surface until they are captured for reuse. Floater balls are a novelty for golfers, but the novelty is short-lived for the staff who must retrieve them.

Practice Facility
Practice Greens

A practice facility is normally defined as any driving range that provides both practice greens for putting and areas for golfers to practice their short game.

Range Markers

Range markers are signs with large numbers that help golfers estimate how far they have hit a ball on a driving range. Some practice facilities mark distances with items such as discarded car tires, large barrels, and flags. I once saw range markers with large cutout targets in the shape of cows.

Bag Drop

A bag drop is an area outside a golf course designated as a spot where golfers may unload their clubs before parking.

Many private clubs and upscale public courses employ attendants who, while players check in at the pro shop, move the players' bags from the bag drop onto golf carts.

Clubhouse

Most of the activity at any golf course—especially before and after a round of golf—takes place in the clubhouse. A typical clubhouse has lockers and rest rooms, full-service dining or some kind of snack bar, and tables or other areas for golfers and their friends to congregate.

Pro Shop
Golf Shop

A golf course's pro shop, or golf shop, is typically connected to the clubhouse, but it may be a nearby, stand-alone facility. Golfers sign up to play (either by phone or in person) at the pro shop, and it is here that they check in prior to play or to take lessons, and where golf merchandise is available for sale. Most pro shops are staffed by a PGA or LPGA professional and his or her assistants.

THE PEOPLE YOU MEET

Amateur

An amateur golfer is someone who plays for fun rather than for profit. An amateur may be a person of any age and any ability level.

Professional

A professional earns her living in some capacity (or combination of them) within the golf profession. Most professionals are members of either (or both) the PGA and the LPGA, the two recognized professional golfers' associations in the United States.

PGA and LPGA
Professional Golfers' Association
Ladies Professional Golf Association

The PGA is the Professional Golfers' Association, which was established in 1916. Today the PGA is mostly composed of men but includes some women. The LPGA, which was formed in 1950, is the Ladies Professional Golf Association. It was created to support women who wanted to become professional golfers.

Club Professional

A club professional is any professional golfer who holds a position at a golf course rather than playing on a professional tour.

General Manager

A general manager, who may or may not be a golf professional, holds the top staff position in a large organization that operates one golf facility.

Director of Golf
A director of golf is a golf professional in charge of all golf operations within an organization that operates more than one course.

Head Professional
A head professional is in charge of operations and staff at one golf course. The head professional may or may not offer lessons.

Director of Instruction
A director of instruction is a teaching professional at one or more golf courses, and is responsible for setting the philosophy of a course's teaching staff and overseeing their teaching activities.

Teaching Professional
A teaching professional is involved almost exclusively with giving instruction.

Assistant Professional
An assistant professional at a golf course is active at some level within the LPGA or PGA and reports to the course's head professional. He may teach or work with golfers in the pro shop.

Master Professional

A master professional is an LPGA or PGA professional who has completed all the requirements for this designation, including a specified number of years of continued membership and service, special projects, and ongoing training.

Starter

A golf course's starter is the person who supervises tee times and tracks play on the course. At many smaller courses, the starter's role is filled by an assistant professional, while many larger courses have a nonprofessional trained to perform the duties of a starter.

Course Designer

Course designers are the architects of golf courses; many become as famous as the courses they design. Rarely is a golf course built without the involvement of an accomplished course designer, landscape architect(s), and other trained professionals. Often golfers—both professionals and amateurs—become involved in course design.

Superintendent

The golf course superintendent maintains the playability of the course. Working closely with the head professional, this person supervises the staff responsible for mowing and irrigating all areas of the course, and those who set hole locations on each green.

Greenkeeper

Many of a golf course's maintenance staff have specific jobs and titles, the most notable of which is the greenkeeper, whose total focus is on proper maintenance and playability of all greens. In many small operations, the course superintendent and the greenkeeper are the same person.

Ranger/Marshal

A golf course's ranger, or marshal, is a staff person or volunteer who drives around the course to monitor the pace of play. The ranger also serves as an observer along the course, providing first aid when needed and communicating any problems to pro shop staff.

Caddie

A caddie is a person who carries a player's bag but does not play while doing so. Caddies were a fixture in the game before the advent of motorized carts, although some private clubs and upscale public courses still have caddie services.

Caddies are required on professional tours because carts are prohibited. They are responsible not only for carrying the bag and helping with club selection but for knowing course yardages. Caddies also serve as lay psychologists; it has become part of their job to keep players focused on the game and to help keep players' emotions on an even keel.

Looper/Loop

Another name for a caddie is looper, because a loop is another name for a round of golf. Perhaps a round is so called because it starts and finishes near the same place— the clubhouse—thus making a loop. Caddies always sign on for a full round—or loop—of golf.

Forecaddie

A forecaddie is a spotter whose role is to find (or spot) balls when they have landed and signal the ball's location. The forecaddie may be assigned to move along the course with the same group of golfers or to stay in one spot—like the 1-hole where the most trouble occurs.

THE EQUIPMENT

Golf Clubs
Set of Clubs

Golf clubs are the implements you use to hit a golf ball. Although they are called clubs, they have been designed to hit only golf balls, nothing else. A standard set of clubs includes eight irons, four woods, and a putter, but any number of irons and woods can make up a set.

Starter Set of Clubs

A starter set of clubs is a partial set intended to give a new golfer a way to take up the game without committing to a big monetary investment. Most of these sets include four irons, three woods, a putter, and a golf bag for a bargain price. Usually the bag bears the name of a little-known manufacturer.

Carry (Number)

To carry means to have a club in one's golf bag, and a golfer may carry up to a maximum of 14 clubs. During a round, if a club is damaged in normal play, it may be replaced. However, a club broken in anger may *not* be used or replaced during the round.

Feeling friendly and want to share clubs with your partner during a round? You can in a partnership competition, as long as the total number of clubs you and your friend carry doesn't exceed 14.

Woods

Woods are clubs that have a fat, rounded head on the side behind the face that strikes the ball.

Fairway Woods

Fairway woods are woods other than the driver that are used when distance from the fairway or more accuracy from the tee is needed.

1-Wood
Driver

The 1-wood, also known as the driver, is the least lofted club in a player's bag and is used to drive the ball long distances off the tee.

Other Numbered Woods
Metals

Other numbered woods include the 2-wood, 3-wood, and so on, to whatever number a player needs to achieve a desired distance. These clubs are known as woods even though the heads on most of them are metal; many golfers call them metals, as in "3-metal," instead of woods.

Utility Woods

Utility woods are becoming more and more common. Many have smaller, lighter-weight heads and/or more loft, and they are designed to get the ball into the air—for example, out of heavy grass or from tight lies.

Irons

Irons are clubs with a flat, bladelike head. About two-thirds of a typical set of clubs are irons, but not all golfers have the same number or type of irons in their bag. Most irons are actually made with steel, graphite, or titanium (iron itself would be too heavy). A normal set of irons includes those numbered 1 through 9, a pitching wedge, a sand wedge, a lob wedge, a gap wedge, and an equalizer.

Loft

Loft is the tilt on a club's face that helps get the ball into the air. The lower the club number, whether it's a wood or an iron, the less loft the face has. The term is also used to describe the flight of the ball. The more loft the club has, the higher the ball will travel in the air, and the less it will roll once it has landed.

Each iron is designed to hit a ball about 10 yards farther than the iron with the next-highest number. For example, if a machine hits the 7-iron from a particular set of clubs 150 yards, then it will hit the 6-iron from the same set of clubs 160 yards and the matching 8-iron 140 yards. Every golfer has to learn his own distance with each club in a set.

Wedges

Wedges are clubs that are used more for accuracy than for distance, and they are commonly relied upon during the last 100 yards of play on a hole. The basic difference among wedges is the amount of clubhead loft.

Pitching Wedge

The pitching wedge has less loft than a sand wedge or a lob wedge.

Sand Wedge

As its name implies, the sand wedge is most often used to hit out of sand. However, many players use it from grassy lies within 80 to 85 yards of the hole.

Lob Wedge

The lob wedge is more lofted, so it is used in a variety of situations where the ball needs to be hit a higher, shorter distance.

Gap Wedge

In most sets of clubs, the loft in each iron is approximately four degrees different from the next numbered iron. For example, the 1-iron has four degrees less loft than the 2-iron, which has four degrees less loft than the 3-iron. The higher the number of the club, the greater its loft.

Traditionally, the pitching wedge and the sand wedge are eight degrees different in loft. To make up for this big difference, which prevents golfers from hitting between where these two clubs would be effective, many manufacturers now offer what is called a gap wedge.

Equalizer

The Equalizer is the name Ben Hogan gave his favorite wedge, and it is the pitching wedge in a set of clubs that bears his name.

Bounce

Bounce refers to the amount of angle between the leading edge (the front of the clubhead) and the contact point of the sole (the back of the clubhead). A club with the correct amount of bounce will allow the golfer to hit a ball from thick grass or soft sand, high and accurately, and with enough spin to land softly on a nearby green. The secret is finding a sand wedge that has the correct angle (anywhere from 8 to 18 degrees) to suit your style of play.

Long Irons

Irons numbered 1, 2, 3, and 4 are called long irons. Their shafts are longer than those of other irons, and they hit the ball farther—or longer—because their clubfaces have less loft.

Short Irons

Short irons are those numbered 8 and 9 and the wedges. They have been given this name both because their shafts are shorter than those of other irons and because they are designed to hit the ball short distances. These clubs have more loft, allowing a golfer to hit the ball higher and with greater accuracy. These clubs are intended for use by all golfers, regardless of their height.

Mid-Irons

Mid-irons are the clubs in between long and short. I mention them as a distinct category for the purposes of this discussion, but they are hardly ever referred to as a separate class of clubs.

Sticks
Tools

Many golfers refer to their clubs as sticks or tools. Someone may say jokingly, "I'll just get my tools, and then I'm off." This usage was probably started by players who wanted to make it sound as if golf requires the precision of a surgeon or skilled craftsman.

Grip
Shaft
Stick
Hosel
Head

All golf clubs have the same basic components. These include the grip, the circular rubber or leather material that enables you to grasp the club. The grip is attached to the top end of the shaft, the cylindrical tube, also known as the stick. Next is the hosel, the part of the club where the shaft enters the head, and the clubhead, the part used to hit the ball.

Face
Toe
Heel
Sole

The striking surface of any club's head is known as its face. The rest of the clubhead goes by names much like the parts of a shoe: the front end is the toe, the back end is the heel, and the underside of the head is its sole.

Grooves

The face of an iron has lines on it known as grooves. The purpose of the grooves is to help add spin to the ball. Specific guidelines in *The Rules of Golf* regulate groove width and depth, and the amount of space manufacturers can put between each groove.

Square Grooves

Square grooves refers to the shape of a groove when viewed in cross section, as opposed to U-shaped grooves. Square grooves are designed to put more spin on the ball, giving the golfer a possible advantage because more ball spin means more ball control. True square grooves do not conform to *The Rules of Golf*.

Flex
Torque
Clubhead Speed

The amount a club's shaft bends is its flex, and the amount its shaft twists is its torque. To hit a golf ball straighter, you need a low-torque shaft. Your clubhead speed (the speed with which you swing the club) dictates your ideal shaft flex. Most players with fast swings use clubs with stiff shafts.

I have learned to be skeptical of a shaft's advertised level of torque or flex. Each golfer needs to find out how a shaft behaves for him, rather than select a club based on how it is marketed.

Springlike Effect

Recent technology has changed the dynamics of golf equipment. Not only does a golf ball compress against the face of a wood at impact, but the face of the club compresses against the ball, then bounces back to its original shape. This action is called the club's springlike effect.

Strong Irons

Strong irons are a club manufacturer's ploy to make the golfer think he's hit a particular iron farther than usual. For example, a strong 7-iron may produce a longer shot because the loft of the clubhead is actually that of a 6-iron.

Investment-Cast Clubs

Club manufacturers use two main methods to create irons: investment casting and forging. Investment casting is a quick process whereby a mold is used to mass-produce identical clubs.

Forged Clubs

Forged clubs are pounded out of raw steel. A longer process than investment casting, forging requires a lot of hands-on attention.

Sweet Spot
Center of Gravity

All clubs have a sweet spot, or center of gravity. This is the point of contact between the clubhead and the ball that results in optimum accuracy and distance.

Perimeter-Weighted

The most popular clubheads in the game today have perimeter-weighted, investment-cast designs that are more forgiving of off-center hits.

Swingweight
Swingweight is defined as the relationship between the weight of the grip and the weight of the clubhead when the two club parts are balanced on a scale whose fulcrum is 14 inches from the head of the club.

Swingweight Scale
Kenneth Smith is the inventor of the swingweight scale, whose measurements range in numbers from 1 to 9 and in letters from A (light) to E (heavy).

Muscle-Back Irons
Cavity-Back Irons
Irons, whether investment-cast or forged, are named for the design of their clubheads. Muscle-back irons have a little bulge of metal on the back side of the head. Cavity-back irons have some of the metal in the center of the clubhead hollowed out. Both types have a lower center/sweet spot that makes it easier to hit the ball effectively.

Offset Clubs
Irons and many woods are made in a design called offset. This design has an abrupt bend at the bottom of the hosel so that the hosel is positioned out in front of the club-face. Offset clubs help straighten out the strokes of golfers whose balls go too far right (right-handers) or left (left-handers).

Putter

Putters are special clubs that have very little loft, as they are designed to roll the ball on the ground and are used almost exclusively on putting surfaces. Putters are usually sold separately, but most starter sets contain one.

Flat Stick
Short Stick

Because the putter is flat, its most common nickname is flat stick, and, because it is usually the shortest club in a set, it is also referred to as a short stick.

Blade Putter

There are four basic styles of putters—end-shafted blades, center-shafted blades, heel-toe weighted models, and mallets. A blade putter can be used by right- or left-handed golfers, as it has a flat surface on both sides of the clubhead.

Mallet-Head Putter

A mallet-head putter is flat on the side that hits the ball and round on the back side. This design stabilizes the putter's head and keeps it square through impact.

End-Shafted
Center-Shafted

There are variations of the two basic types of putter, classified by where the club's shaft connects to the head.

Those with shafts at the back of the putter are called end-shafted, and those with shafts in the middle are called center-shafted.

Navel Putter
Belly Putter

A navel, or belly, putter has a long shaft that allows a player to anchor the club at the midsection (near the waist) of his body and to move the putter like a pendulum. Since the player's body is helping to hold the putter in place, his hands can be used solely to guide the swing of the club.

Heel-Toe Weighted

Heel-toe weighted putters allow golfers to strike balls off center and still hit them solidly, just as perimeter-weighted irons do.

Heel-toe weighted putter design was made popular when Karsten Solheim introduced his Ping Anser in the late 1960s. Now the most widely used putter head style among amateurs and professionals alike, the design works because its weight distribution puts more mass in the clubhead's toe and heel, which guards against the head twisting during the stroke.

Knockoff Clubs

Knockoff clubs are cheap copies of name-brand clubs, much like some goods in the designer clothing business.

Some knockoff clubs are of a good quality, but many are not, so buyer beware. I've had good results with a knockoff driver that I picked up a few years ago from my father.

Custom Clubs
Club Fitting

Custom clubs are just what the name implies—clubs designed specially for an individual player. As you can tell from the number of terms for clubs, there are many different designs on the market.

Just as a pair of shoes should fit your feet so that you walk comfortably, golf clubs should suit your build and your swing. A trained club professional can measure your height, swing speed, proper lie angle, grip size, shaft length and flex, then order a set that suits you.

Buying a Game

A golfer who purchases anything new on the market—gimmicks or standard equipment—is said to be buying his game.

The Finishes of Clubs

In years past, all ladies' clubs had blue grips and the heads of woods were always blue, often with little butterflies on them. However, clubs now come in many colors, with flat, shiny, even iridescent finishes, so both men and women can order a standard club in their favorite finish, color, and design. Ladies can even get black clubs, and men can get clubs in pastel colors with flowers on them if they choose.

Golf Ball
Rock
Pellet

A golf ball is a ball uniquely designed to be used in the game of golf. Rock and pellet are casual names for a golf ball.

Wound Golf Ball
Two (or More)-Piece Ball

The terms wound and two (or more)-piece refer to what is inside a golf ball and how it is constructed. The classic wound golf ball has a core wrapped with what look like very thin rubber bands. The two (or more)-piece ball has a center core with at least two layers of synthetic materials fused around it.

Dimples

Dimples are the depressions on a golf ball's surface. Without dimples, a golf ball wouldn't fly nearly as far. Golf ball manufacturers constantly experiment with different materials, construction methods, size, shape, and dimple patterns.

Compression

When someone asks if you're playing a 90 or a 100, he's interested in the amount of compression in the golf ball you use. Compression is a manufacturer's term for how much pressure it takes to flatten the ball. Flattening the ball allows it to rebound off of the face of the club, which creates its amount of distance.

Generally, harder hitters and faster swingers want a higher-compression ball, whereas slower swingers—such as many seniors, youngsters, and those new to the game—may do better with lower-compression balls. Today's golf balls have compressions ranging from 80 to over 100.

Balata
Smiling Balls

Balata and surlyn refer to golf ball covers. Most professionals and experienced amateurs use balls with balata covers, which are softer and tend to make the ball more responsive. One drawback of a balata ball is that when it is hit improperly, its cover may scuff. These scuff marks may be slightly rounded, like a smile, and thus these golf balls are commonly referred to as "smiling" balls.

Surlyn

The surlyn cover, introduced by Ram in 1968, is more durable and cut-resistant. Many amateurs and other people who have to pay for their own golf balls prefer surlyn-covered balls because they last longer.

Sleeve of Balls
Numbers on Balls

Golf balls have traditionally been sold in sleeves. Typically, a sleeve contains three balls of the same type, brand name, compression, and number (for example, a sleeve of 1's or a sleeve of 8's). The numbers are useful only for telling you which balls came from the same sleeve; for example, in a box containing a dozen balls, you'll usually get a sleeve of 1's, a sleeve of 2's, a sleeve of 3's, and a sleeve of 4's, or four sleeves with balls numbered 5 through 8.

A friend who watched me play for years had always wondered why I used balls with any number in normal play but all the balls I used in tournaments bore the number 3. She was greatly disappointed when she finally found out that there was no significance to this numerology other than my own superstition.

Logo Balls

Logo balls bear a company's identification mark for promotional purposes. Collecting balls with different logos has become a popular hobby with many golfers.

Limited-Flight Balls

Limited-flight golf balls are specially made to fly about 70 percent as far as a normal ball. They are used on outdoor ranges that are too short for regular balls hit by long hitters, and at many indoor ranges where balls are hit into a restraining net.

Cayman Golf Balls

Cayman golf balls are designed for short courses. The dimples on a Cayman ball are more like pimples—they are rounded, not depressed. A Cayman ball flies about half the distance of a normal golf ball.

Experienced Balls

Experienced balls is a marketing term for used golf balls, like those found on a golf course and turned in at the pro shop. Experienced balls are commonly offered for sale in pro shops at a discount price.

X-Outs

X-outs are new golf balls that have not met the construction standards of their manufacturer. These balls, which are typically sold at a reduced price, are so called because they are marked with one or a series of large X's that obscure the name of the manufacturer.

Tee
Peg

A tee is a wooden peg, about 2 to 2½ inches long, with a concave top and pointed bottom. It is used to raise the ball off the ground at the teeing ground. A tee is often called a peg.

Ball Marker

A ball marker is used to identify the location of a ball on the green so that the ball can later be placed in the same spot. A golfer can use anything small, flat, and round (like a coin) as a ball marker. Most ball markers have a small nub on the bottom for easy pushing into the ground. Some golf gloves have a snap attached at the wrist, half of which is a ball marker.

Every pro shop sells ball markers. Many of the markers sold at these shops are mementos bearing the name and/or logo of the course. I treasure the hundreds of ball markers I have collected all over the country and around the world, especially those from memorable courses played in Hong Kong, Japan, Korea, and Scotland.

Divot Fixer
Divot Tool
Ball Marks
Pitch Marks

A divot fixer, also called a divot tool, is a two-pronged piece of metal or plastic used to repair depressions in the green caused by hard-hit balls. These divots are also called ball marks or pitch marks.

Divot tools are readily available in pro shops to encourage golfers to repair divots wherever they find them and regardless of who was responsible for them. Repairing divots is an example of proper golf etiquette.

Golf Glove
Cadet Glove

A player wears a golf glove (on the left hand for right-handed golfers, on the right for lefties) to help prevent blisters and to reduce hand perspiration that might cause the player to let go of the club accidentally. Other players wear a golf glove simply because someone advised them to. One junior golfer told me she liked to wear a glove simply because it was "cool."

Golf gloves come one to a package in men's, women's, and junior sizes from small to extra large. Cadet gloves are designed for players with short fingers and wide palms.

Headcovers

Headcovers are designed to fit over the heads of woods to prevent the clubheads from banging against one another in the golf bag. You can buy them individually or in sets of three or four. Typically, headcovers sold in sets are imprinted with numbers so that a golfer can identify a wood by looking at its cover.

Headcovers come in all shapes and materials. Many collegiate golf teams provide players with a single headcover bearing a likeness of the school's mascot. I know one golfer who has a set of headcovers shaped like animals. Anyone who has watched a televised tournament in which Tiger Woods is playing has probably seen his tiger headcover.

Cleats
Spikes

Cleats, also called spikes, is the name for the nubs on the bottom of golf shoes that prevent a golfer from slipping during a swing. In the past, most spikes were made of metal; the majority of today's spikes are made of plastic.

Soft Spikes
Spikeless

Soft spikes do less damage to the sensitive grass on golf greens (and to clubhouse carpeting) than do metal spikes. Spikeless golf shoes have very small, soft spikes or bumpy rubber soles with no spikes at all.

Carry Bag

A carry bag holds clubs and is light enough, even when full, to be carried by hand. In today's game, it is the most popular style of bag used. Players on high school and college golf teams are required to use carry bags.

Staff Bag

The large, heavy bags that caddies carry for tour players are called staff bags. Staff is another word for employee. Most staff bags advertise the name of the club manufacturer whose products the player endorses.

Cars
Carts

Many golfers get around the golf course in motorized cars or carts, which are either gas-fueled or electric, are designed for a driver and one passenger, and have storage room on the back large enough for two sets of clubs.

On most courses carts are not required, and golfers may choose to walk. However, some courses—especially those with hilly terrain and long distances between greens and tees—require players to use carts.

Pullcarts
Trolleys

Pullcarts are like narrow baby strollers, but most have only two wheels and one handle, and are wide enough for only a small golf bag. Pullcarts are designed to operate very much like luggage on rollers, and many golfers prefer pullcarts to carrying a bag by its shoulder strap.

In Great Britain, pullcarts are called trolleys. In some countries, including the United States and Japan, many pullcarts today are motorized and can be run by remote control. As you walk from one point to another on the course, these pullcarts carry your clubs nearby.

Cart Paths

Cart paths are narrow passageways on a course on which golf cars and carts travel. Some cart paths are paved, some are gravel, and some are just dirt and mud. In Scotland, there are even cart paths made of crushed oyster shells.

90-Degree Rule

Some courses require that you keep your golf cart on the path at all times and carry the club(s) you will use to your ball. Other courses allow driving anywhere on the course, except within 30 feet of tees and greens. Many of these courses request that you drive along the cart path to a point even with your ball, then drive straight from the path to the ball and straight back to the path. This is known as the 90-degree rule.

GETTING READY

Scorecard
Yardage

Most golf courses provide their own scorecard. A scorecard may or may not contain a picture or a map of the course, but virtually all scorecards provide information about each hole, such as yardage and par.

The yardage of most par-3 holes is up to 250 yards from men's tees, 210 yards from women's tees. Par 4's are from 251 to 470 yards for men, 211 to 400 for women; par 5's range from 471 to 690 for men, 401 to 590 for women; and the rare par 6 is 691 yards or more from men's tees and 591 yards or more from women's.

Local Rules

A golf course's local rules take into account conditions that are specific to that course. Local rules can usually be found on the course's scorecard.

One example of local rules comes from a course near Sea-Tac Airport, south of Seattle, Washington. The course has rules governing what players can do if their ball lands near one of the airport towers (which happen to be located in the middle of the course). There is no local rule at that course, however, for when a low-flying 747 on approach causes you to mis-hit.

Teaching Aids

A teaching aid is any device used by a player to improve his game or by an instructor to demonstrate proper technique. The following are examples of teaching aids: videotape of a golfer's swing, mirrors placed so that a golfer can see his own form, and clubs weighted in such a way as to correct a swing. Aids are being invented all the time.

Squeeze Time
Starter Time
Tee Sheet

Squeeze time and starter time are terms used by a golf course's staff to refer to scheduled tee times that help control the pace of play when there are several groups waiting to begin. Typically, these times are simply noted on a tee sheet and are not assigned to any particular player or group.

Single
Twosome
Threesome
Foursome

These are common terms for the number of golfers playing together in a group. Threesome and foursome also refer to specific games of golf. To learn more about them, see "Clubhouse Chatter" under "Amateur Tournaments and Games Golfers Play."

Lineup

Before you begin a round, the starter will tell you to play away or will announce the order in which all players—or groups of players—tee off at the first hole. This announcement is called the lineup.

The starter usually announces a group as the "X party" ("X" being the last name of the golfer who signed up for the tee time), very much like a dinner reservation at a restaurant.

On the Tee

A player or group that is on the tee is at the first tee and ready to begin play.

On Deck
In the Hole

The second person or group waiting to proceed to the first tee is said to be on deck. The third person or group in line to play is said to be in the hole.

Starting Time
Tee Time

When you call for a starting time, or tee time, you will most likely be assigned a time that doesn't fall exactly on the hour or half hour. Starting times are scheduled at 8-minute, 10-minute, or 15-minute intervals, depending on the pattern of play at the course. Don't be surprised if you get a tee time of 10:28 or 2:36.

Your tee time is the precise minute you are to appear at the first tee. This means you are stretched, warmed up, and ready to play, with your glove on, a ball and tee in your hand, and the club you've decided to use out and ready. It is not the time you show up to pay your fees.

Walk-On
Standby

If you have no tee time and just show up, hoping to be able to play, you are a walk-on, or standby. Be prepared to wait.

You are now ready to proceed to the first tee.

Tee
Talk

146 Terms Often Used at the Start of Play

HANDICAPS AND RELATED TOPICS

Handicap

The handicap is golf's way of allowing people of unequal ability to compete against one another. It is defined as the average number of strokes over par an amateur makes during one 18-hole round. (We can think of handicaps this way, but the actual formula for figuring out handicaps is much more complicated than this.) For example, a golfer who scores 10 strokes over par for several rounds has a 10-handicap. An official handicap is based on the best ten 18-hole scores out of the last twenty 18-hole rounds a golfer plays. For the purposes of determining handicaps, scores from two 9-hole rounds can be combined to arrive at an 18-hole score.

Most adult male golfers have a handicap of around 16, whereas most adult female golfers have a handicap of around 28. Professionals do not have handicaps.

Home Course
Away Course

Where you play most often is known as your home course, and any other course you play is an away course. The process of updating your handicap scores is much easier—almost automatic—at your home course; one reason is that the process is always overseen by the same people.

Temporary Handicap

Some players use a temporary handicap, based on their scores in five 18-hole rounds.

Handicap Card

Golfers carry a handicap card, which shows their home course handicap and what scores have been used to determine this handicap. Golfers' handicaps are updated monthly. A golfer hopes to lower his handicap through continued play.

Handicap Index Number
Handicap Differential

The handicap card also lists a handicap index number, which is created with a complex formula. In simplistic terms, a handicap is not an even number but rather a decimal, like 15.9 instead of 16. When you visit an away course, your handicap is translated into an appropriate number for that course, and it may be different if the away course is much more difficult or much easier than your home course.

This is how your handicap index number is formulated: The course rating from the tees you played in your last 20 rounds of play is subtracted from your score in those same 20 rounds. That number is multiplied by 113—the standard slope rating—then divided by the course's slope rating. The resulting number is your handicap differential on that course.

To get your handicap index number, the best 10 of these differentials are first averaged, then multiplied by .96. This index number is based on your best scores, not your average scores, so you aren't expected to consistently score this well.

Course Rating

A course rating is the score that the USGA has determined scratch golfers should shoot when playing on that course from a specific set of tees and under normal conditions.

Slope Rating
Slope of the Course

Each course has a slope rating, which is the measure of the difficulty of the course as compared to other courses. This is also called the slope of the course. A slope rating of 113 means the course is of average difficulty. A score higher than 113 means it is more difficult than average, and a score lower than 113 means it is easier than average.

Post a Score for Handicap
GHIN System
Golf Handicap Index Network

Every time an amateur golfer plays a round (either 9 or 18 holes), he is required to record, or post, a score on a computer located at the course. The score can then be used along with his previous scores to compute his handicap. The system that is used to compute handicaps is called GHIN, which stands for Golf Handicap Index Network.

Equitable Stroke Control (ESC)
Adjusting for Handicap

A golfer's handicap should not change significantly because of one bad day. Equitable stroke control (sometimes written ESC) is a fancy name for the help a golfer gets—for handicap purposes only—if he has an unusually high score in one round of play.

This procedure, known as adjusting for handicap, allows the golfer to post only up to a maximum score on any hole, based on his handicap. All courses have a chart that golfers can use to arrive at their ESC. Your local golf professional can help you determine the correct ESC based on your handicap.

Course Handicap

Every hole on every golf course has a handicap rating, too. This is called the course handicap. Each hole's level of difficulty is rated in relation to every other hole on that course. The easiest hole is ranked 18, and the most difficult is ranked 1. These rankings are shown on the course scorecard.

Gross Score
Net Score
Handicap Strokes/Pops

Gross score is defined as the total number of strokes a golfer makes in a round. Net score is the gross score minus handicap strokes, also called pops. For example, an 18-handicap golfer who shoots a gross score of 90 receives a net score of 72 (i.e., 18 subtracted from 90).

Plus Handicap

Most handicaps are *subtracted* from gross scores to get a net score. However, a player carries a plus handicap when her gross score is lower than par almost every time she plays. This handicap is added to the player's gross score to arrive at a net score.

Scratch Player

Amateur players who average par on every round are called scratch players.

Strokes Where They Fall

Strokes where they fall refers to a style of play in which players receive all handicap strokes but one at a time, hole by hole. So if a golfer's handicap is 5, she receives one stroke off each of the five most difficult holes of the course.

Roll Off the Low

Roll off the low is a simplified way of keeping score when using handicaps. For example, if there are three players in a group and one has a handicap of 5, one 10, and one 15, the one with the lowest handicap plays as a scratch player (receives no handicap strokes, or pops), the 10-handicap golfer receives 5 strokes, and the 15-handicap receives 10.

Single-Digit Handicap

A golfer with a single-digit handicap is quite simply anyone with a handicap between 1 and 9. There's a story in golf lore about a nongolfer who, after hearing that a player had a single-digit handicap, attempted to figure out which finger the golfer was missing.

PLAYING A ROUND

Front Nine
Back Nine

The front nine are the first nine holes one plays in an 18-hole round, usually begun at the first tee. The back nine are the second nine holes of play, starting at the 10th tee.

Opening Hole
Finishing Hole

The first hole you play, regardless of its number, is called your opening hole, and the last hole you play is your finishing hole.

Turn Time
Making the Turn

Any golf course may give you a turn time before you begin a round of play. If you are playing an 18-hole round, the turn time is the time the course believes you should have completed the first nine holes and be starting play on the back nine. This is also called making the turn.

Out
In

Out is used to refer to playing the front nine (holes 1 to 9) of an 18-hole course. In refers to playing the back nine (holes 10 to 18). In tournaments, for example, a player may be said to have "gone out in 34 and come in in 36, for a total score of 70."

Many golf courses were designed so that play on the first nine holes proceeded out (away) from the clubhouse to the farthest point of the course, and play on the second nine holes proceeded back in. In recent years, courses have been designed in such a way that players can conveniently make a visit to the clubhouse—for snacks, rest stops, to replace lost golf balls, etc.—after the front nine holes.

Partner
Pairings

Another golfer on your team is a partner of yours, and you play as teammates. Groups of players in a tournament are called pairings. Pairings may be groups of two, three, four, or more, depending on the tournament.

Competitor
Fellow Competitors

In golf, the term competitor refers specifically to a player in a stroke-play competition. Those who play in the same group (or in other groups in the same competition) with a competitor are called fellow competitors.

Teeing Ground
Tee Up

The starting point for every hole of golf is the teeing ground. A player tees up a ball he is preparing to hit by placing it in the teeing ground; he may or may not use an actual tee.

A tee may *not* be used anywhere on a golf course except the teeing ground. For example, you can't tee up a ball on a fairway, in a hazard, or on a green without incurring a penalty.

Tee Markers
The Blocks

Tee markers define the specific area where a golfer can start play on each hole. There are usually three sets of tee markers—in different colors and placed in different spots. Tee markers are also called the blocks because in many courses they are made out of blocks of wood.

At the start of a round, players decide which color tees they will play, then play the entire round teeing off from the same color tee markers.

Forward Tees

The forward tees—those closest to the hole and that allow a golfer to play the course's shortest possible total yardage—usually have red tee markers. Most women play the red tees, but they are not required to.

Middle Tees

The middle tees on each hole usually have white tee markers. Traditionally, men play the white tees, although they are not required to.

Back Tees

The back tees on each hole offer players the greatest challenge off the tee because they are the farthest tees from the hole. Most male professional golfers play the back tees.

Senior Tees
Junior Tees

Many courses have tees located ahead of the forward tees that make for a short course. Called senior tees and junior tees because of the players that typically use them, these tees are painted a gold color.

Championship Tees
The Tips

Championship tees mark a hole's longest distance off the tee and are used for tournaments. These tees—which are usually black—are located behind the back tees. Another name for these tees is the tips.

Named Holes

Some holes have distinctive names as well as numbers. For example, you may hear a commentator say a player is about to play Pine and Thistle instead of holes 8 and 9. A hole may be named after flowers, landmarks, or some other feature of the surrounding landscape.

Raining on Their Tee Party

From the story of the Mad Hatter, raining on their tee party is a play on words used when rain begins to fall on a group of golfers who are on the tee.

Mulligan
Do-Over

In a friendly game of golf, a mulligan is a free shot granted to you by your partners when a previous shot is poorly played. If the mulligan is also poor, you still have to play it. Do-over is another name for mulligan.

Finnigan

A finnigan is played after a poor mulligan. You get to play whichever of the two shots is better.

H-T-H

H-T-H means "hit 'til happy." In other words, the golfer may hit as many shots as she wishes until she likes the result and that's the ball she continues to play.

H-T-H isn't seen in most serious games, and it is prohibited in tournaments. However, Arnold Palmer was observed offering the H-T-H option to one of his amateur partners during a pro-am tournament in the summer of '99.

Shotgun
Shotgun Start

A shotgun, or shotgun start, is a way of getting many people to start play at the same time. By using all (or many) of the holes of the course as a starting point rather than just the first tee, groups of golfers can start and finish a round about the same time.

Everyone starts at their assigned tee, then moves through the course to finish on the hole just before the one where they began play—that is, instead of playing from hole 1 to hole 18 on an 18-hole course, you might shotgun from hole 18, then play hole 1 on through and finish on hole 17.

Stroke Play
Medal Play

In stroke play, the strokes taken by each player are counted and then totaled at the end of the round. The player with the fewest number of total strokes is the winner. This type of play used to be called medal play.

Whiff

When a golfer attempts to hit a ball but misses, he is said to have whiffed. Unfortunately, whiffs count as a stroke in any golf game.

Match Play
Halved (the) Hole
All Square
Holes Up
Dormie

Match play is a golf game in which two or more people compete against each other on a hole-by-hole basis. The lowest score on each hole wins. Regardless of the score on a hole, a player can lose only 1 point—or one hole—at a time. For example, if golfer A shoots a score of four on the first hole and golfer B shoots a score of seven on the same hole, golfer A wins the hole.

When players tie for low score on a hole, they are said to have halved the hole. If the players have won the same total number of holes, they are all square. Whenever one player is ahead of the other, the golfer in the lead is said to be however many holes up.

Dormie is a match-play term used when one player is ahead in the match by the same number of holes that remain to be played. For example, a player who is ahead in a match by two holes with only two holes left to play is said to be dormie.

Bingo-Bango-Bongo

Bingo-bango-bongo is a game for two or more players with different levels of ability. Each hole is worth 3 points.

A bingo (1 point) is earned when the first golfer in a group gets his ball on the green of the hole being played. A bango (1 point) is earned by the golfer whose ball is closest to the hole after *all* of the group's balls are on the green, regardless of the number of strokes it took each golfer to get there. A bongo (1 point) is earned by the first player in the group to get a ball into the hole.

For the bongo point, the player whose ball is farthest from the hole putts first. If that player's ball doesn't go in the hole, the player whose ball is now farthest from the hole putts. This order—farthest ball first—continues until a player sinks a putt. The game winner is the player with the highest number of points at the end of the round.

Nassau

Nassau is a game in which two opposing players each try to win 3 possible points. The front nine are worth 1 point, the back nine are worth 1 point, and the total score for the full round of 18 holes is worth 1 point. For scoring purposes, either gross or net scores may be used.

The winner is the player who gets at least 2 points. For example, golfer A has the low score on the front nine and wins 1 point. Golfer B has the low score on the back nine and wins 1 point. Golfer A's 18-hole total is lower, so she is awarded 1 point. Golfer A is the Nassau winner by a score of two to one.

6-6-6

6-6-6 is a game for four players. One player is matched against one of the other players for holes 1 through 6, switches to another opponent for holes 7 through 12, then takes on the final player for holes 13 through 18. The player who wins the most holes wins the match.

3-3-3

3-3-3 is exactly the same as 6-6-6, except that it's played over nine holes, with a new match beginning after every three holes.

Skins Game, Friendly Skins

A friendly skins game is the same as a professional skins competition, but the stakes aren't as high and either gross or net scores can be used. Two to four golfers may compete. The low score on each hole wins a skin. Skins can represent points or a dollar amount.

When two players tie for the low score on any hole, the skin or skins for that hole carry over to the next hole. When a hole is finally won, the player who wins the hole gets the skins carried over plus the one for that hole.

SETTING UP

Grip (Holding the Club)
Baseball, or 10-Finger, Grip

A grip is the way a golfer puts his hands on a golf club. A player who uses the baseball grip, also known as the 10-finger grip, has all 10 fingers in contact with the club, similar to how a baseball bat is typically held.

Vardon Grip
Overlap Grip

The Vardon grip was made popular by Harry Vardon, a well-known amateur golfer in the early 1940s. Harry, a right-handed golfer, held his club with the little finger of his right hand overlapping the left hand in between the index and middle finger. This grip is also called the over-lap grip.

Interlock Grip

Right-handers who use this grip interlock the little finger of the right hand with the index finger of the left hand (vice versa for left-handers). Made famous by Jack Nicklaus, the interlock grip is recommended for golfers with small hands.

Strong Grip
Weak Grip
Neutral Grip

Regardless of the way a golfer holds—or grips—a club, there are different positions for the hands. These positions include the strong grip—the hands are turned away from the target, top hand palm down, bottom hand palm up; the weak grip—the hands are turned toward the target; and the neutral grip—the hands are positioned straight up and down. All three of these ways of positioning the hands can dramatically affect the way a ball is hit.

Choking Up (or Down)
Grip Down

Some golfers gain more control of their club by choking up on the club, which means they place their hands on the lower part of the handle, closer to the clubhead. This is also called choking down, or gripping down, on the club.

Harley Grip

The Harley is an exaggerated grip in which three or four knuckles of the top hand are on top of the grip, the palm almost facing the ground. It is called the Harley because it looks like a motorcycle rider's grip on his accelerator. Typically, a golfer uses this grip when he wants to quickly turn the clubface at impact.

Club Selection

Deciding which club to use as you prepare to make a shot—from any spot on the course—is called club selection.

In-Between Clubs
Half-Club Long/Short
Underclubbed

Club selection is dictated by the distance the ball has to be hit. When a ball misses the desired distance by about five yards—long or short—the player is said to be in-between clubs.

This is also called hitting a half-club long or a half-club short. For example, if your 7-iron lands the ball just short of the target, you can assume that your 6-iron might have gone just past the target.

A golfer is underclubbed when she selects a club that cannot reach within 10 yards of the desired target.

Take Less Club

To take less club means selecting a club with more loft so that you hit the ball shorter than the actual yardage to the hole. When playing a hole that is located downhill, for example, you might need to take less club to avoid overshooting the target.

Take More Club

Sometimes course conditions or design reduce the distance balls fly, and to reach a target a player should take more club than the distance normally dictates. For example, an uphill hole may necessitate using a less lofted club to get the distance needed to reach the hole.

Preshot Routine

A golfer's actions prior to hitting a ball are called his preshot routine. A preshot routine may include actions such as gripping the club, standing behind the ball to determine the correct aim, walking up to the ball, setting the club behind the ball, assuming a stance, and taking a practice swing.

A preshot routine should be consistent in every respect. Many experts believe that consistency in the preshot routine leads to consistency in the swing.

Muscle Memory

Muscle memory is an often used, but technically incorrect, term that refers to a player's attempt to develop a consistent swing. A player's brain is actually responsible for developing a consistent swing, and the brain relays the correct information on this swing to the muscles in the body.

Setup
Address the Ball
Stance
Grounding the Club
Soling the Club

The setup is the body's position in relation to the ball before the ball is hit. A golfer addresses the ball after he has taken his stance, or set his feet, but prior to swinging the club. Addressing the ball also includes grounding—or soling—the club, which is placing the bottom of the clubhead on the ground behind the ball.

Whenever I explain addressing the ball to clinics of new golfers, someone always smiles as he faces the ball, plants his feet, and, with a wave of his hand, says, "Hi, ball."

Square Clubface
Target Line
Closed Clubface
Open Clubface
Club Wide Open

Having a square clubface means that the leading edge of the clubhead is perpendicular to the intended target line. The target line is the direction in which you want the ball to go.

There are three other clubface positions at address. The first—the closed clubface—is used to make the ball hook (for a right-handed player, a hooked ball goes left).

This is achieved by rotating the club so that the leading edge of the clubhead points to the left (for a right-handed golfer) of the target line.

To add more height (loft) to the flight of the ball or to slice the ball (hit it right), a right-handed golfer opens the clubface. That means he places the club so that the heel is in its normal position, rotating the toe of the club to the right.

The clubface position known as club wide open is used to hit out of sand. A right-hander aims the bottom edge of the clubface far to the right of the target by swiveling the toe of his clubhead back to the right, leaving the heel in its normal position.

Hooding the Club

If a player wants his ball to fly lower and roll as far as possible after it lands, he should keep the bottom front edge of the clubhead perpendicular (at a right angle) to the target on the horizon, moving his hands with the shaft of the club forward of the ball throughout the swing. This is called hooding the club.

Lay-Back Club
Laid-Back Clubface

Lay-back club and laid-back clubface both refer to an action that a golfer takes to give more loft to his club so that the ball flies higher than usual and rolls less after it lands. After the golfer aligns the leading edge of his clubhead at a right angle to the target on the horizon, he moves his hands and the shaft of the club away from the target.

Square Stance
Closed Stance
Open Stance

When a golfer addresses the ball in a square stance, both of his feet are even and parallel with each other as they point toward the ball. However, in a closed stance, the feet are not parallel; a right-handed golfer's feet point slightly to the right of the target (the hole). The right-handed golfer's left foot is forward of the right foot; the left-handed golfer's right foot is forward of the left. An open stance is just the opposite of a closed one.

Aim

When players discuss aim in golf, they are talking about where the face of the clubhead is pointing before and during the swing.

Alignment

Alignment refers to setting up a player's body position and clubface aim in relation to the target. For right-handed golfers, the body should be aligned parallel, just left of the target line, rather than aimed directly at the target.

Waggle
Sitting Down
Dipping

The waggle is a body movement—designed to help loosen and relax the golfer—made just prior to hitting the ball. Many golfers are taught to stick their seats out to help them avoid sitting down, or to squat with their weight back over their heels to keep their weight from shifting too far forward. Golfers who sit and pop back up again during the swing are said to be dipping.

ABOUT SWINGING

Swing
Backswing
Downswing
Forward Swing
Follow-Through

The swing is the act of hitting a golf ball with a club. The backswing is the first movement of the club, when the golfer moves the club back and up from the ball to what is called the top of the swing. The golfer then moves the club forward to hit the ball. This is called the downswing.

The forward swing is when the club moves from the point of impact with the ball and toward the target. The forward swing gives way to the follow-through.

The follow-through is the only part of the swing motion that is sustained—usually while the golfer watches the flight of the ball. It assures that the golfer completes the swing instead of stopping it midway. This offers the golfer time to stay in balance and a moment to pose—probably one of the reasons why there are so many photographs of golfers in the follow-through position.

Full Swing
Swing Plane

There are several kinds of golf swings. The full swing is used to get maximum distance on any shot, most often when driving the ball off the tee or approaching the green from farther than 100 yards away. All other swings are abbreviated and are used to make shorter shots such as pitch shots or chip shots.

Golfers hope to maintain a constant swing plane, which is the angle of the club in relation to the body, from the starting position through the backswing and downswing.

Baseball Swing
Flat Swing
Upright Swing

A golfer makes a baseball swing, also called a flat swing, when he moves the club around his body on the backswing, keeping his hands well below his shoulder line at the top of the swing.

An upright swing is one whose downswing, forward swing, and follow-through form a shape like the letter V.

Reverse C

Reverse C is an old-fashioned swing position in which the golfer's body, viewed from the side, resembles a backward letter C at the completion of the swing. This swing motion is no longer recommended.

Laid-Off Swing

The term laid-off swing is used to describe the position of a golfer's left hand (or right hand for a left-handed golfer) at the top of the backswing, when the palm of the hand is almost horizontal to the ground. The position of the club at the top of the backswing is laid flat, which makes it difficult to get the club back into proper position to hit the ball.

Caddie Swing

A caddie swing is a swing that does not resemble any known form but usually gets the job done; most are self-taught or mimicked. I am told that this term was first used during the 1930s when most caddies were local children who learned to golf by watching the players for whom they caddied.

Practice Swing

Golfers frequently take a practice swing before getting into their stance for the real thing. The purpose of a practice swing is to get a feel for the actual shot. Too often a player makes a great practice swing, but the actual swing leaves a lot to be desired.

Lag
Loading the Club

If you watch a golfer's swing, you'll notice that his wrists are hinged (bent back) at the top of his backswing. Lag refers to how long the wrists stay hinged on the downswing before unhinging to allow the clubhead to align with the hands at impact. When golfers hinge their wrists, they are said to be loading the club. The more hinged the wrists, the more loaded the club. In golf, lag is a good thing.

Release

Release refers to the action of unhinging the wrists on the downswing of the club.

Lag Time

The length of time a golfer's wrists stay in the hinged position during the downswing is called lag time. The more lag time, the more power the golfer generates.

One-Piece Takeaway
Handsy

One-piece takeaway describes a golfer's backswing when his arms, shoulders, and club move away from the ball as a single unit. Swings are said to be handsy when they rely on the hands more than the shoulders—that is, there's a lot of hand rotation and little or no shoulder turn.

Upper-Body Swing

A swing that is characterized by little or no foot, leg, or hip movement is an upper-body swing.

Sway
Reverse Weight Shift

Sway is undue lateral movement of a golfer's body during a swing. Golfers are taught to move their body weight to the back foot during the backswing, then shift to the forward foot through the downswing. However, in a reverse weight shift, the golfer's weight shifts toward the target in the backswing and away from the target in the downswing. This usually produces poor shots.

Casting the Club
Fishing from the Top
Throw the Club from the Top

Casting the club and fishing from the top describe when a golfer's wrists unhinge—flipping from a bent-back to bent-forward position—at the top of the backswing and just before the start of the downswing. The usual result is that the ball doesn't travel as far as it should.

To throw the club from the top does not mean literally to throw the club; it is simply another phrase for casting the club or fishing from the top.

Forward Press

A forward press is a slight motion a golfer makes with his hands to move the shaft of the club slightly forward and toward the target just before beginning his backswing.

Flying Elbow

When a golfer's nontarget arm (the right arm of a right-handed golfer, the left arm of a left-handed one) moves away from his body at the top of his backswing, making his elbow point out rather than down at the ground, he is said to be guilty of a flying elbow.

Drive
Tee Shot

Hitting a ball from the tee, regardless of the club used, is referred to as a drive, or tee shot.

Big Dog
"Let the Big Dog Eat"

Big dog is a nickname given to the driver. When a golfer wants his drive to be a long one, he might say, "Let the big dog eat."

Tee Off

At last, it's time to tee off! This term is used to describe driving the ball from a tee. It is also used, a little less precisely, to refer to the time a player began a round, as in "We teed off at 9:30."

"Fore!"

"Fore!" means "Look out!" and "Duck!" If you think there is a possibility that a ball in flight will hit someone, yell "Fore!" with purpose.

When you hear "Fore!," *duck and cover your head.* Having been hit eight times by a golf ball, I've decided I must have a big target painted on me. Being hit by a ball is an experience to avoid because it leaves a lasting impression.

Have a great round of golf!

Links
Lingo

327 Terms Frequently Heard Along the Course

TERMS FOR GREAT DRIVES AND FAIRWAY SHOTS

Ace (the Shot)
Aced the Hole

A drive from the tee that goes into the hole is referred to as an ace. The golfer is said to have aced the hole.

Aced It

Aced it is a term that is most often heard on a long-yardage hole (par 4 or 5) when a drive goes a long way down the fairway and lands in a great spot.

Blue Bayou (Blew by You)

When a player drives a ball that lands near another player's ball but rolls quite a ways past it, it might be said that the drive "blue bayou" (for "blew by you").

D-S-P/Dead Solid Perfect
T-Q/Tournament Quality

D-S-P is an abbreviation for dead solid perfect, and T-Q means tournament quality. These terms describe shots that go in the intended direction and to the intended area—in other words, shots that feel great to the player and sound and look great to everyone nearby.

Didn't Hold Back

It is said of a player who made an effective shot with maximum effort to make the ball go the greatest possible distance that he didn't hold back.

Good Pass at It

When a ball travels long and straight toward the target *and* the player who hit it looks good—through the swing to a balanced finish—the player is said to have made a good pass at it (the ball).

Grip It and Rip It

A player has gripped it and ripped it when he has hit the ball far by keeping a tight hold on the club and executing a powerful, if not necessarily balanced, swing.

Hammered It

A player has hammered it when his shot has gone a great distance.

Busted It

A player who makes a shot—usually a drive—that goes very far, very long, and very straight has busted it.

Hit It Flush
Flushed It

When a player hits a ball very well—with maximum distance and in the desired direction—and the shot feels good to the player, he is said to have hit it flush or flushed it.

Hit It Pure
Pure Shot
Textbook Shot

When a ball goes far and straight and the shot feels good to the player who makes it, the player is said to have hit it pure or hit a pure shot. This is often referred to as a textbook shot.

Laced a Shot

Laced a shot is a term that means the same thing as aced a shot and hit it flush. In other words, the term is used when a golfer hits a shot very well.

Let the Shaft Out

A golfer who has let the shaft out has hit a great shot—most often a drive off the tee—that looks good and has unusually good distance.

Nailed It

Nailed it means hitting the ball solidly, far, and straight.

Nothing Left in the Bag

A player who believes that he could not possibly have done anything better on a shot of a certain distance may say that he has nothing left in the bag. Arnold Palmer had nothing left in the bag when he drove the par-4 first green in the 1960 U.S. Open at Denver's Cherry Hills.

On the Screws

A shot hit really well, most often from the tee, may be said to have been hit on the screws. The term comes from the days when real woods (rather than metals) were widely used and clubface inserts were held in place by screws. A shot hit right in the center of the clubface—where the screws were located—usually produced good results.

Ripped It

A golfer has ripped it when he has hit a great shot really far. The term usually refers to a drive from a tee.

Striped It

Many fairways are mowed lengthwise from the tee to the green, producing what looks like a series of stripes. So when a golfer makes a drive from the tee that is long and straight and lands right in the middle of the fairway, he is said to have striped it.

TERMS FOR NOT-SO-GREAT SHOTS

Airmailed the Green

When a player hits a ball intending for it to land on the green but, instead, hits it so hard that it flies past the green, he has airmailed the green.

"Ball Is Wet"

When a ball is destined for a water hazard, players may be overheard to say, "That ball is wet," even before the shot hits the water.

Balloon Shot

A balloon shot is one hit almost straight up in the air, much like a helium-filled balloon that is let go. Unlike a balloon, a balloon shot has very little distance and comes down quickly.

Belly the Ball
Blading the Ball
Blades

To belly the ball means to hit it near the middle with the leading edge of an iron. Think of a golf ball with an equator line. When a clubface meets the ball right on that imaginary line, the result is a ball that flies lower and farther than desired.

Irons are sometimes called blades, so hitting the ball in this spot is also called blading the ball.

Blocked Shot
Flared Shot

A blocked shot is one that goes to the right (for a right-handed golfer) because the player holds the club tight and doesn't allow his hands to turn. The blocking of the club can also create a flared shot, which sends the ball straight for a short distance, but then curves to the right.

Came Out of the Shot

A golfer who came out of the shot is one who—prior to hitting the shot—straightened up partially, then tried to hit from this position. A ball hit this way never does what the golfer intends.

Chunk It
Hit It Fat

A golfer is said to chunk it—or hit it fat—when his club hits the ground before hitting the ball and creates a divot, barely making contact with the ball itself.

Chili Dip

A chili dip is a short pitch shot—with a swing that is nearly straight up and down, not back and forth—that is hit fat.

Cooked It

When a golfer hits a ball that goes farther than she intended, she is said to have cooked it.

Duffed a Shot

A player who misses an easy shot might be said to have duffed the shot.

Errant Shot

An errant shot is one that doesn't go in the direction the golfer intended.

Fluffed It

When a club hits the grass instead of the ball, making the ball pop straight up, then land in almost the same spot it was in before being hit, the golfer has fluffed it.

Flyer
Jumper

A flyer (or jumper) shot occurs when grass gets caught between the clubface and the ball, affecting the amount of spin on the ball. The result is that the ball travels farther than the golfer thought it would and doesn't stop when the golfer thought it should.

Forced the Shot

When a player tries to hit a club farther—for example, by hitting harder or faster—than his experience and ability allows, he has forced the shot.

Fresh Air

Fresh air means the same thing as whiff—that is, the player misses the ball completely. The shot is called fresh air because the swing causes a little breeze.

Got Ahead of It

When a golfer moves just before hitting the ball so that his body is forward of the ball but his hands and club remain behind it, it is said that he got ahead of it. This mistake usually results in a shot similar to a slice.

Got Cute with a Shot

When a player attempts to save a stroke by hitting a tricky shot, it is said that she got cute with the shot.

Goin' Fishin'

A player is goin' fishin' when he hits his ball into a lake or pond.

Heeled It

When a club makes contact with the ball close to the heel of the clubface—where the shaft enters the clubhead—the player has heeled it. This term is the opposite of toed it.

Hit a 300-Yard Drive

A player is kiddingly said to have hit a 300-yard drive from the tee when she hits the ball almost straight up into the sky rather than forward. It is a 300-yard drive because it goes 100 yards up, 100 yards out, and 100 yards down.

Hit It Heavy

Hit it heavy is the same as hit it fat. Both terms refer to the golfer's club hitting the ground behind the ball so that the ball doesn't go very far.

Hung It Out to the Right

When a ball stays right of the target in flight and lands to the right, never moving left to the target, the golfer is said to have hung it out to the right.

In Jail
In the Log Cabin
In the Furniture

A golfer is in jail when he has hit the ball into trees whose trunks resemble jail bars. The player is not expected to get out of the trees with only one shot. This situation is also called being in the log cabin or being in the furniture.

Leaked Right

When a shot aimed and hit directly at a target goes slightly to the right of the target, the shot is said to have leaked right. (Note: Usage is restricted to balls that veer right; a similar shot to the left of a target is not said to have leaked left.)

Mis-Hit
A mis-hit occurs when a golfer does not hit the ball well and the shot is way off target.

Pop-Up
A pop-up is a shot—in most cases from the tee—that goes up in the air to almost the same height as the distance it flies forward, similar to a pop fly in baseball that doesn't leave the infield.

Pull
Yank
Pull and yank describe shots that veer left of the target (for right-handers) or right of the target (for left-handers) immediately after being struck. You'll often hear a golfer mutter, "Oh, darn, I pulled it," or "I yanked it!"

Push
Push describes a ball that starts out going right (when hit by a right-hander) or left (when hit by a left-hander) of the target. A push is the opposite of a pull.

Reload
A player who hits a ball out of bounds or to a location where it can't be found is required to hit another ball

from the same spot where the previous ball was hit. When this happens, the player is said to reload. Penalties are assessed for reloading according to *The Rules of Golf*.

Rider

A shot that is hit far enough along the fairway that the player finds it worthwhile to get in his golf cart and ride to it is jokingly called a rider.

Shank
Sherman Tank

When the hosel of a club contacts the ball rather than the clubface, the shot is called a shank. A ball that is hit with a hosel, which is a rounded surface, inevitably travels way off target. Some golfers, in the belief that merely using the term shank will cause them to shank a ball, prefer the term Sherman tank. Whatever works.

Shipwrecked

When a golfer is playing well, looking good, and feeling great about her game during a round, only to see her game suddenly fall apart, she has been shipwrecked. When this happens, the golfer rarely recovers her game during that round.

Skank

Any lousy hit is a skank. No one wants to skank it.

Spraying the Ball

A golfer who can't hit the ball straight and whose shots fly off in different directions is said to be spraying the ball.

Thin Shot
Skulled Shot
Take No Turf

When a golfer hits only the ball and takes no turf, he has hit a thin shot. A skulled shot is a type of thin shot in which the ball has been hit squarely on what could be referred to as its forehead. The ball flies with less spin, going much farther than desired and rolling quite a distance after landing.

Toed It

When a ball hits off the toe of the clubface rather than the middle, the golfer is said to have toed it. The resulting shot is usually a short one that misses the target.

Topped Shot

A topped shot is one where the clubhead contacts the top half of the ball instead of the bottom half. A ball that is topped rolls instead of becoming airborne. This is one of the most common mis-hits in golf.

U-B-U
Ugly but Useful

A poorly hit ball that doesn't look good but nevertheless goes the desired direction and distance is called a U-B-U, short for ugly but useful.

Wheels Came Off

Sometimes a golfer is playing very well and making low scores, but suddenly she starts hitting the ball everywhere except at the target. Her stroke total soars and she finishes the round with a very high score. When this happens, it is said that the golfer's wheels came off.

OTHER KINDS OF SHOTS

Approach Shot

An approach shot is a short shot whose purpose is to land the ball on the green, preferably close to or in the hole.

Bump-and-Run

A bump-and-run is a short shot, usually to a green that is located on high ground above where the player is standing when making the shot. The player tries to hit the ball so that it will first hit the side of the hill—the bump—which slows the ball down so that it can run onto the green.

Chase It Up

A chase-it-up shot lands in front of the green and continues to roll—and roll—until it finally stops on the green. The player who hit the shot runs toward the ball while it's rolling—or chases it up—to see where it stops.

While playing at St. Andrews in Scotland, I asked my caddie what club I should hit to try to make it to the green, which was about 200 yards away. He said, "Because the ground is hard, hit a 3-iron and chase it up, Mum."

Anyone who has ever played St. Andrews knows you should always listen to your caddie there. I did, and he was right!

Chip Shot

A chip shot is made with a medium-lofted club (often a 7-iron) near the green and is hit so it will pop into the air and run across the green to the hole.

Pitch Shot

A pitch shot is like a chip shot in that it is executed with a medium-lofted club and its purpose is to put the ball on the green, but it flies higher and rolls less after it lands. If it has enough spin on it, it may even back up.

Chop
Woodcutter Shot

Chops and woodcutter shots are used to get balls out of bad lies in bunkers. A golfer hits the sand behind the ball hard with a downward chopping motion in an attempt to blast the ball out of the bunker.

Cut Shot

A cut shot is made with an angled swing that gives the ball both sidespin and backspin. This shot is used to make the ball go high in the air and land softly with little roll.

Dead-Hands Shot

A dead-hands shot is hit with little or no wrist action and almost no acceleration during the downswing. A well-executed dead-hands shot will land *very* softly after only a short flight.

Dead Shots

Almost any shot that goes beyond what the player intended can be described using the word dead. For example, a ball that curves too far to the right might be described as going dead right. Similarly, a great straight shot is said to be dead straight.

Bunker Play
Explosion Shot

Bunker play refers to shots made to get a player out of a sand trap (i.e., bunker). The explosion shot is an example of bunker play; it is a shot that hits the sand behind the ball rather than the ball itself, in the hope that the displaced sand will carry the ball out of the bunker. This shot is named for all the flying sand, not for the force required to execute the shot.

Finesse Shot
Delicate Shot

A finesse shot is one that is hit from a difficult lie (for example, from behind a tree, out of very thick weeds, or from water), requires talent and imagination, and has rarely if ever been tried by that player. A finesse shot is also called a delicate shot.

Massage the Ball

When a player hits a short shot that requires a lot of finesse and hits it so accurately that it's almost as if she picked up the ball and threw it to the target, she is said to have massaged the ball.

Flip Wedge

A flip wedge is an approach shot made a short distance from the green. The golfer uses a wedge club in an attempt to literally flip the ball onto the green.

Floater Shot

A floater shot is one hit with very little clubhead speed so that the ball barely spins in flight, may seem to float in the air, and does not travel very far.

Flop Shot

A flop shot is one hit so that the ball gets into the air quickly, doesn't travel very far forward, and lands softly, like a high jumper doing the Fosbury Flop. This shot is typically used to get the ball over a bunker or other hazard to reach a pin located close to the near edge of the green.

Greedy Chip

When a golfer attempts a difficult chip shot from off the green rather than a safe shot to set up a short putt, he is making a greedy chip shot. This shot is often counterproductive because it tends to go past the hole to a spot from which it is difficult to sink a one putt.

Inside-Out Swing

An inside-out swing may be done either accidentally or on purpose. The hands stay close to the body on the backswing, and the downswing moves at an angle away from the body—rather than across the body and in line with the target. A right-handed golfer's ball goes right of the target.

Outside-In Swing

An outside-in swing usually makes a right-hander's ball go left of the target. The backswing goes almost directly back from the ball rather than curving behind the golfer's body, and the forward swing cuts across the ball from right to left.

Over-the-Top Swing

When a golfer uses only the top half of his body to swing the club, with little or no leg movement, the swing is said to be over the top. This swing takes a right-hander's club left of the target, which means the ball veers left of the target.

Knockdown Shot

A knockdown shot is a movement of the club that a golfer does intentionally to get the ball to fly lower than it normally would and to stop more quickly. To execute this shot, a golfer reduces the loft of the clubface and abbreviates the follow-through.

Punch Shot

A punch shot is the same shot as a knockdown shot, but it is more explosive. Typically, a golfer uses a punch shot when playing into the wind.

Knuckle Shot

A knuckle shot is made with an abbreviated backswing and little, if any, wrist hinge, the knuckles of the target hand (the left hand of a right-handed golfer, the right hand of a left-handed golfer) facing the ground during the swing. There is little hand action in this stroke, and when executed at about three-quarters the speed of a normal swing, it produces a lower, more penetrating ball flight—perfect for keeping the ball below the wind.

Lay-Up Shot
Lay-Back Shot

The lay-up (or lay-back) shot is used to land the ball just short of an obstacle—an especially useful shot when you are faced with an obstacle that would require a well-struck ball to get past. The trick is to select a club that will allow the ball to reach a point just in front of the obstacle.

Pick It Clean

A golfer who makes a shot without hitting any turf at all, only the ball, is said to have picked it clean. This may be an intentional shot—for example, hitting out of a bunker without taking any sand—or it may be accidental.

Recovery Shot

A recovery shot is one that gets a golfer out of trouble—for example, from a bad lie—and into better position, perhaps saving a stroke or two in the process.

Risky Shot

A shot is risky when it might result in a higher score if it is not hit perfectly. In many cases, the reward for hitting a risky shot may not outweigh the penalty for missing it. In the movie *Tin Cup*, the character played by Kevin Costner missed a crucial risky shot.

Safe Shot

A safe shot involves no risk. Every hole is designed to produce a score of par when it is played by making safe shots. An example of making safe shots is playing a dog-leg in two shots rather than trying to cut it.

Soft Shot

A soft shot is one hit with little or no spin so that the ball lands as if it has fallen on a pillow and barely rolls at all.

Feathered It

When a player hits a shot that seems to fly gently into the air and lands lightly—like a feather—he is said to have feathered it.

Trap the Ball

A golfer traps the ball when she intentionally keeps her hands and the shaft of her club forward of the ball to lessen the effective loft of the club. A trapped ball may fly lower and have more spin than normal.

SHOTS THAT CURVE LEFT OR RIGHT

Hook

A hook is a shot that travels way left (if the player is right-handed) of the intended target during flight. There are several reasons why a ball hooks, but the most common one is too much sidespin on the ball at impact.

Duck Hook
Draw

A duck hook is a shot hit with so much sidespin (right to left for right-handed golfers) that the ball begins by traveling forward, then takes an almost 90-degree left turn—

rarely the golfer's intention. A draw is a shot hit with a little sidespin; the ball curves gently in flight from right to left (for right-handers).

Slice/Fade
Banana Ball

For a right-handed golfer, a shot that goes far right is a slice. Because of the curve the ball takes in flight, a slice is sometimes called a banana ball. (For left-handed golfers, a slice goes to the far left.)

For a right-handed golfer, the same shot to the right but with less curve in flight is a fade. (As with the slice, a less pronounced curve to the left is a fade for left-handed golfers.)

Wicked Slice

A wicked slice is a shot that is so uncontrolled it goes far to the right of the target (for right-handed golfers), landing *way* off line and possibly in a hazard or out of bounds. A left-handed golfer's wicked slice goes far left.

Sweeping Hook

A sweeping hook is a shot that first travels far wide of the target, then flies gently back toward the target and lands in a good spot. A sweeping hook is a shot made by design, and it may take years to perfect.

Shaping a Shot

Getting a ball to curve gently in flight is called shaping the shot. This is a particularly helpful skill when you are trying to reach pins that are tucked into the side of a green.

Working the Ball

A deliberate attempt to make a ball fade or draw, or hook or slice, is called working the ball. It takes years of practice to perfect this skill. Most professional golfers have the ability to draw or fade the ball on command.

OTHER TERMS: FROM ADVICE TO PLAYING IN THE WIND

Advice

How appropriate that this term should follow explanations of the many shots golfers make. Advice is any suggestion given to a golfer that might influence how he plays. Advice is not always helpful.

In tournaments, golfers are permitted to take advice only from their caddies or playing partners.

Aerated Fairways

Many golf course maintenance crews have machinery that punches holes in the turf to expose the soil to air, which creates aerated fairways. The plugs of soil that are left behind are an annoyance for a few days afterward, but aerating is necessary to keep the grass healthy.

Grain
Against the Grain

Look closely at certain types of grasses and you will see that the blades all point in the same direction; this is called the grain of the grass. When you putt with the grain, you hit the ball in the direction the grass is pointing. When you putt against the grain, you hit the ball in the direction opposite to the direction the grass is pointing, which means you have to hit the ball harder than you do when you putt with the grain.

Awkward Stance

A golfer is said to have an awkward stance when she is unable to place her feet level on the ground; one foot is on higher ground than the other, making balance during the swing difficult.

Bail Out

To bail out means to hit away from the target to avoid some kind of trouble, usually in the hope that the ball will land in a more desirable spot for the next shot.

Ball Flight
Trajectory

Ball flight is the path—forward, right, or left—of the golf ball in the air. Trajectory is the upward angle of the ball's flight and the height a ball reaches when hit with a specific club.

Launch Angle

Launch angle is the angle a ball's flight path makes with the ground immediately after being struck. Launch angle is determined to a large extent by which club is used and how well the ball is hit.

Ball in Play

The ball with which a player tees off becomes the ball in play and remains in play until it has been holed out. If a ball is lost or hit out of bounds between the tee and the hole—or a player simply wishes to use a different ball—the replacement ball becomes the official ball in play.

Wrong Ball

According to *The Rules of Golf*, a provisional golf ball or any other ball that is not a player's ball currently in play is known as the wrong ball.

Ball Is Sitting Down

A ball is sitting down when it comes to rest in a spot where it is hidden by the grass around it.

Ball Retriever

A ball retriever is a gadget used to get balls out of water. It looks like a telescoping pool stick and has a snatching mechanism on the end.

Ball Washers

Ball washers are devices that clean golf balls, commonly found near teeing grounds. They often resemble old-fashioned hand water pumps with cleaning brushes that the golf ball is plunged down into.

Ball Won't Fit

When a golfer says the ball won't fit, he means he believes the fairway is so narrow that it is virtually impossible to hit the ball accurately enough for it to land within the space available.

Big Ball
Little Ball

Big ball is the planet earth, and little ball is the golf ball. This usage is commonly heard when a golfer hits the earth prior to hitting the golf ball.

"Bite"

When a golfer sees his ball going past the spot where he wants it to stop, he may command the ball to "bite."

Blind Shot
Blind Hole

A blind shot is one hit when the target can't be seen. When that target is the hole, it is called a blind hole.

Elevated Green

An elevated green is a putting surface that is located higher than the golfer's vantage point on the fairway or the tee. Depending on the design of the hole, a player may or may not be able to see the flag or the position of the hole as she makes an approach shot.

Hidden Pin

A hidden pin is a hole whose location can't be seen by a golfer from the fairway. The hole may be obscured by an obstacle, such as a tree.

Tucked Pin

A tucked pin is a flag that is hidden behind a high bunker or other obstacle that has been placed in front of an elevated green.

Bogey Train

When a golfer makes a score of 1 over par on a series of holes, he is said to be on the bogey train.

Bunker
Greenside Bunker
Sand Trap
Trap

A bunker is a sand-filled hazard. A greenside bunker is found adjacent to a green. Bunkers used to be known as—and are still commonly called—sand traps, or simply traps. Most people know and use the terms trap and sand trap, although the terms are not recognized in *The Rules of Golf*.

The Beach
Sandbox
Kitty Litter Box

The beach, sandbox, and kitty litter box are all slang terms for a bunker, or sand trap.

Fried Egg

A fried egg is a ball embedded in a bunker, sitting in a pocket of sand. The term came about because of the way the ball resembles a sunnyside-up egg in a frying pan.

Burn

Burn is a Scottish word for creek. This term is rarely used to refer to the creeks in U.S. golf courses, but it is often used by commentators during the British Open and other tournaments played in the British Isles.

Carry Distance
Total Distance

Carry distance is how far a ball travels in the air before it lands. Total distance is a ball's carry distance plus the distance it rolls after landing.

Cart Golf

You are playing cart golf when you share a cart with another player and you both manage to hit your golf balls near each other. This causes less wear and tear on the course and makes efficient use of the cart.

Casual Water

Casual water is an accumulation of water, other than a hazard, from which a golfer may take relief.

Relief

Moving a ball out of an area from which a player is not required to play is called relief. For example, a player may take relief when his ball lands in an area marked as "casual water" or "ground under repair."

Free Relief

When a player is not penalized for moving his ball, it is called free relief. In most cases, however, a penalty is assessed for taking relief.

Take a Drop

A player can take relief by going through a process called taking a drop. The player marks and picks up the ball, holds it in an outstretched hand at shoulder height, and drops the ball to the ground. The specific circumstances of the errant shot dictate whether a player may take a drop and how many (if any) penalty strokes are assessed.

Caught a Break

When a bad shot ends up in a good position, the golfer has caught a break. An example is a shot that hits a tree and bounces into the fairway.

Check Up

A ball is said to check up when, because of backspin, it stops and then backs up a bit after landing.

Club for Duff

When a player needs to hit over an obstacle (for example, a water hazard) and is trying to decide what club to use, it may be best to club for duff or choose a club that hits far enough that even a poor hitter—like a duffer—could clear the obstacle.

Colored Stakes
Colored Lines

A golf course may be marked in various areas with a combination of colored stakes and colored lines. Based on *The Rules of Golf*, the color of a line or stake indicates whether a player can shoot in (or from) that area.

Course Management

Course management is the process of determining how to get through a course in as few strokes as possible. To be successful at course management, a golfer has to take into account factors such as proper club selection for shots of various distances, ways to compensate for her game's strengths and weaknesses, and how she is hitting the ball on a particular day.

Distance Control
Dialing in Clubs

A golfer has distance control when he knows how far he hits with each club. Knowing the potential of each club is not unlike turning the dial on a combination lock to open a safe, so golfers call it dialing in one's clubs.

Divot

The piece of turf dislodged when a golfer makes a shot is called a divot. Contrary to what many think, a divot is created from the turf in front of the ball, *not* from behind it. Virtually all shots other than putts produce at least a small divot; the biggest divots are those made by iron clubs.

Golf etiquette dictates that golfers repair their divots. Many golf courses provide grass seed, fertilizer, sand, and soil for this purpose.

Dogleg (Left or Right)

A dogleg is a turn in the fairway between the tee and the green; it can be either a left or a right turn. When viewed from the air, the turn looks much like the angle in a dog's hind leg. Most doglegs are part of the design of the course's architect and are meant to increase the level of difficulty of the course—and, consequently, a golfer's sense of satisfaction for playing the course well.

Cutting the Dogleg

When a player attempts to bypass a dogleg by going for the green from the tee rather than playing the hole the way it was designed to play—one shot to the dogleg and another to the green—he is said to be cutting the dogleg.

Dropkick

A golfer is said to execute a dropkick when his club hits the ground before touching the ball. Most golfers do not attempt to perfect this type of shot.

Duffer

Duffer is a slang term for a golfer who is not very good. The term is most commonly used to describe oneself, not someone else. My dad has a mat outside his home that says, "Duffers Welcome." A friend of mine taught her three-year-old to say, "Daddy's a duffer golfer." The dad was not pleased.

Hacker

Computer hackers are known for their skill, but a hacker in golf is a duffer with a jerky swing to boot.

Chopper
A chopper is a golfer whose swing looks like that of someone trying to chop down a tree with an ax.

Embedded Ball
A ball that has landed with such force that it has become at least half buried is called an embedded ball.

Entry to the Green
The entry to the green is the path a ball takes to reach the green. One of every golfer's challenges is to find the best entry to the green for his approach shot. When there are no obstacles between the ball and the hole, the player has a good entry to the green. When there is no easy shot—for example, if the shot has to go over a bunker or a water hazard—the player has a bad entry to the green.

Opening to the Green
The opening to the green is the area (20 to 30 yards or so) immediately in front of the green. Golfers look for good openings.

Narrow Opening to the Green
Big/Wide Opening to the Green
A player has a narrow opening to the green when there are obstacles—bunkers, trees, bushes, rough, and so on—that limit the amount of space she can hit into.

When there are no obstacles in the way, the player has a big, or wide, opening.

Etiquette

The manners, sense of politeness, and honesty with which you play are known as etiquette. Etiquette encompasses many types of activities, some of which are discussed in this book. Two examples of good golf etiquette are being quiet while another player makes a shot and not walking in another player's putting line on the green.

Fairway
The Deck
Driver off the Deck

Although fairway is not an official term in golf, it is the most common name for the short-mown area between a tee and its green. The deck is a slang term for fairway. Playing a driver off the deck is difficult even for accomplished golfers, so average players should heed the advice "don't try this at home."

Fairways in Regulation
F-I-R

A statistic called fairways in regulation, abbreviated F-I-R, tells golfers how well they are driving the ball from the tee. Most 18-hole courses have 14 opportunities to hit a fairway in regulation (because par-3 holes have no fairway and a standard course has four par-3 holes).

Missing Fairways
Found the Fairway

A player who constantly winds up anywhere but in the fairways is said to be missing fairways. A shot is said to have found the fairway when it lands in the fairway after appearing to be headed for trouble or into the rough.

Firm Fairways

A course that has been baked by the sun or has not been watered for a while may have firm fairways, which feel hard underfoot and resist being compressed by golfers' shoes.

Balls roll farther on firm fairways than on normal fairways. Some golfers—for example, those who don't hit the ball far—like firm fairways for precisely this reason.

Soggy Fairways

Fairways that have become waterlogged, owing either to overwatering or rain, are called soggy fairways. Even balls hit hard—or with a long-distance club like a driver— barely roll after landing on soggy fairways, and balls with high trajectories may actually sink into the ground.

Tight Fairways

A fairway that is fewer than 25 yards wide in most places is considered tight. Looking down a tight fairway from the tee, a golfer may not believe she can hit a ball so that it will land within the fairway. The term "ball won't fit" is heard often on a tight fairway.

Fairway Bunker

Any bunker found in the fairway, regardless of its design, is called a fairway bunker.

Pot Bunker

A fairway bunker that has a deep, rounded bottom—much like a pot—with the top edge flush with the terrain is called a pot bunker.

Waste Bunker

A waste bunker is a bunker created out of a patch of ground that is difficult to maintain or where grass won't grow. It provides a better landing area and hitting surface than would exist on that spot if the bunker weren't there. A waste bunker may be located almost anywhere on the course.

Waste bunkers are easily identified. Most are not as well maintained as other areas of the course, and none include a rake for cleaning up after you've hit your ball. There is no penalty for grounding your club prior to hitting out of a waste bunker.

Flippy-Wristed

Some older golfers describe their younger counterparts with the lighthearted but somewhat derogatory modifier flippy-wristed. The term refers to the more flexible, harder-hitting, and better all-around play of the youthful set.

Foot Wedge
Kicksie

When a player's ball is in a difficult lie, another player may suggest that he use a foot wedge—or literally kick the ball to move it to a better spot. A ball moved in this manner is called a kicksie. Of course, this is not a legal move, but golfers often wish that it were.

Forgiving Club

A forgiving club is one that produces good results even when the ball hits off the toe or the heel of the clubhead. Most clubs that are considered forgiving are perimeter-weighted.

French Drain

A French drain is a thin trench on a golf course for conducting rainwater and excess water from the course's irrigation system. Most French drains are filled with pebbles about four to six inches wide and anywhere from a few feet long to the length of a fairway. A ball that lands in a French drain may be moved without penalty.

Get Home in Two (or Three or Four)

To get home in two means that, from where a ball lies and taking into consideration the player's ability and the length he hits the ball, the player should be able to get the ball onto the green with two shots. Likewise, a player can get home in three (or four and so on).

Good Out

A player who manages to get out of trouble—by hitting his ball from a bad location or position to a good one—is said to have made a good out.

Gorse

Gorse is a very prickly bush native to Scotland that grows wild and is part of the rough on many golf courses. It is something you want to avoid!

Grass Bunker

Grass bunkers are not considered hazards, although they are designed to make play more challenging. These depressions are generally smaller than regular bunkers— although most are large enough to stand in—and are lined with grass instead of sand.

Grinder

Being called a grinder is a compliment. A grinder is a golfer who consistently makes the most of her ability. She might not hit the ball as far or as straight as other golfers, but she gets the most out of every shot. A grinder has the ability to get out of difficult spots and often scores well. Like the tortoise in the fable, the grinder wins because of her continuous, persistent effort.

Grounding a Club (in a Hazard)

Grounding a club means placing the sole of the clubhead on the ground before hitting the ball. A player may not ground his club prior to playing out of a bunker or other hazard, with the exception of a waste bunker.

Ground Under Repair
G-U-R

Areas on a course marked as ground under repair present abnormal playing conditions because they are either under construction or have been torn up to make way for improvements. Golfers often use the abbreviation G-U-R to refer to these parts of a course. When playing from these areas, remember to follow *The Rules of Golf*.

Hardpan

Hardpan refers to areas of a golf course (other than greens) where the grass is brown and the ground is dry. A player hitting on hardpan usually strikes more of the ball because the ground beneath the ball cannot absorb the force of the club's blow.

Has No Shot
"You're Dead"

When a golfer has no shot, the ball has landed either in a spot where the line of flight to the green is obstructed or in a spot that literally prohibits the golfer from swinging. A golfer who has no shot may be told by someone else, "You're dead."

Hazard

A hazard is an obstacle on a course anywhere between the tee and the green that has been specially designed to challenge the golfer's ability to reach the green. Hazards may contain water or sand, and players should consult *The Rules of Golf* to determine appropriate play for them.

Drop Area
Drop Box

When a shot lands in a water hazard, the player may be permitted to make his next shot from a spot near the hazard known as a drop area (or drop box). Most drop areas are marked with white paint; if there is no drop area marked, the player must determine where to drop a ball in compliance with *The Rules of Golf*. A player who is forced to play a shot from a drop area is penalized one stroke.

"Hit Down on the Ball"

A player having trouble getting his ball airborne may be instructed to "hit down on the ball." Many golfers take this command literally and swing almost as if they were pounding a spike into the ground, not realizing they are being asked to swing the club along the ground past the ball. This type of swing lets the ball roll up the face of the club before beginning its flight, which results in greater loft.

Put Juice on It
Pinching the Ball

To put juice on it is to hit the ball with lots of spin and hit it well. Juice is a golfer's term for spin. Hitting the ball and the grass at the same time, called pinching the ball, creates spin.

Helicopter

A golfer who throws a club in anger so that the club spins around in flight, making the sound of an airborne chopper, is said to have executed a helicopter.

"Hit It, Hunt It, Hole It"

The phrase "hit it, hunt it, hole it" is a simplified description of how the game of golf should be played. It is commonly said to a player felt to be overanalyzing his game.

Holes Play Long/Short
Course Plays Long/Short

A hole is said to play long when it seems to be farther than it really is, forcing a golfer to play it as though its distance is much greater. A hole plays short when it seems closer than its actual distance and must be played that way. These changes in the apparent distance of a hole can result from weather conditions, changes in the hardness of the ground, the direction of the hole (up- or downhill, for example), or any combination of these factors.

When the same conditions affect apparent distance over an entire course, it is said that the course plays long or short.

Honors
Ready Golf

Honors is golf etiquette for allowing the player with the lowest score at the end of each hole to tee off first on the next hole. The player with the second-lowest score tees off next, then the player with the third-lowest score, and so on. If two players tie for low score on a hole, whoever held honors on the hole before the tie goes first again.

Honors on the first hole of a round is determined by draw, by tournament seeding, by flipping a coin, or by any other method players decide to use. Honors also determines who plays first on shots between the tee and the hole. The player who is farthest from the hole plays first, the second farthest plays second, and so on. Honors continues until all players have holed out.

Ready golf is an informal method of play where honors is disregarded. Instead, whoever is ready first plays first throughout the round.

Hot Balls
"Ball Came Out Hot"

Some golfers play only with a certain brand of balls that they believe are "hot balls"—that is, balls that seem to fly farther than any other ball on the market.

The term hot is used in other ways as well. A player who is doing well during a round may give credit for his success to his "hot" golf balls. Or a golfer might say of a shot that went farther than expected that the "ball came out hot."

Idiot Marks
Sky Marks

Idiot marks are the scuff marks on top of a wood club caused by hitting underneath a ball on the extreme upper part of the clubface. A less offensive term for the same thing is sky marks, a reference to the fact that the shot causes the ball to fly skyward.

Impact
Moment of Truth

Impact is the collision of the clubface and the ball. Another term for impact is moment of truth.

"It's Your Hole"

When playing partner golf, a player who is struggling and who seems likely to shoot a high score on a hole may say to his partner, "It's your hole," meaning he doesn't want his score on the hole to count toward the team score. The partner then knows he should do his best to salvage the hole for the team.

Ladies' Aid

Sometimes a ball lands on a cart path and bounds forward along the path toward the green, getting more distance than the shot deserved. This is called ladies' aid. This term is now used for a shot by either a man or a woman, but it originated in the days when most women golfers rarely hit for distance.

Landing Area

Golf course architects design places where golf balls should land along fairways and on greens. Each of these is a landing area, less noticeable on regular courses than on target courses.

Lay-Up Hole

Some courses are designed with lay-up holes, which are holes that force golfers to avoid an obstacle by making a short extra shot known as a lay-up shot.

Water Hazard

A water hazard is any open water—such as a lake, pond, river, or creek—found on a golf course. Special rules apply for playing a ball that lands in this kind of hazard.

Lateral Water Hazard

A lateral water hazard is one that is located on either side of the fairway or green in such a way that golfers are not required to hit over it. Lateral water hazards pose problems only for golfers who have already hit off target.

About Lies

Lie

Where a golf ball comes to rest on or near the golf course is called the ball's lie. What follows are the 17 most-used terms for describing how a ball is sitting on the course.

Bad Lie

A bad lie is any spot that makes hitting the next shot difficult. For example, a ball that lands in an old divot, in a hole, behind an obstacle, under a bush, or against a rock is said to be in a bad lie.

Bare Lie

A ball that is sitting on a spot with very little or no grass, or where there is only dirt, is in a bare lie.

Bird's Nest

A ball that comes to rest in heavy grass, positioned so that it looks like an egg in a bird's nest, with the grass fanning out around the ball, is said to be in a bird's nest lie.

Buried Lie

A ball that seems to have been swallowed up after landing, nearly or completely covered by grass or sand, is said to be in a buried lie.

Clean Lie

A ball has a clean lie if it is sitting in full view, on nice grass, and in a spot from which it will be easy to make good contact with it on the next shot.

Downhill Lie

A ball has a downhill lie when a right-handed golfer has to place his left foot lower than his right foot when preparing to hit the ball.

Embedded Lie
Plugged Lie

A ball that remains in the exact spot in which it lands—with no roll upon landing—is said to be in an embedded lie, or a plugged lie. This is often caused by grass that is so thick or soft it holds the ball in place.

Fluffy Lie

A ball that is perched on the tips of the grass blades is in a fluffy lie.

Flyer Lie

A lie that causes a player's club to hit grass before hitting the ball—so that grass gets caught between the ball and the clubface—is called a flyer lie. This type of lie usually results in a shot that has less spin and greater distance than the golfer intends.

Good Lie

A ball that is ideally positioned—on the fairway or elsewhere—for the golfer's next shot is said to be in a good lie. A good lie is the same as a clean lie.

Hanging Lie

A ball that has come to rest on an incline and seems to be suspended, with little turf supporting it, is in a hanging lie. Making effective shots from this type of lie is difficult.

Sidehill Lie

A ball in a sidehill lie is either above the player's feet, which makes a baseball-type swing necessary, or below the player's feet, which forces the golfer to crouch to hit it. Either is a tricky shot to play.

Squirrelly Lie

A lie that is so unusual that it causes a player to scratch her head as she ponders how to hit from that spot is said to be squirrelly.

Tight Lie

A ball that has landed in grass that is cut extremely close to the ground is said to be in a tight lie. The ball won't sit up on the grass because there just isn't enough of it. Instead, the ball seems to hug the ground.

Unplayable Lie

If a player determines that making a shot from where his ball rests is impossible, the ball is in an unplayable lie.

Uphill Lie

A ball has an uphill lie when a right-handed golfer has to place his left foot higher than his right foot when preparing to hit the ball.

This concludes our discussion of lies. Just know that there are often more lies in the clubhouse than out on the course.

Line of Play

The direction a player wants his ball to travel after hitting it is known as its line of play. Where the ball actually goes is often another matter.

Lip of the Bunker
Small Lip
Big Lip

The lip of a bunker defines the bunker's area; it is where the bunker's sand meets the surrounding grass. The edge of a shallow bunker is called a small lip. The edge of a deep bunker is called a big lip; getting the ball over a big lip and out of the bunker can be a challenge for a golfer.

Loose Impediment

A loose impediment is defined by *The Rules of Golf* as a natural (as opposed to man-made) object found on a golf course. No object that is growing or otherwise attached to the ground may be considered a loose impediment, nor can an object that is buried solidly in the earth or does not adhere to the ball. Check the *Rules* to find out which loose impediments you are permitted to move from your path.

Lost Ball

A ball is considered lost when it cannot be found in the five minutes a golfer is permitted to search for it.

"There's a Lot of Golf Left"

When a golfer has not scored well over the first few holes of a round, his playing partners may say to him, "There's a lot of golf left." This statement is intended to reassure the poorly performing golfer that he still has plenty of opportunity to improve his score.

Lunchpail-Packing Par 5

Lunchpail-packing par 5 describes a hole that is long and takes a while to play—the implication being that anyone playing the hole should bring along food in case they get hungry.

Markers (Yardage on the Course)
Yardage Markers (on the Course)

Some courses have large color-coded or numbered disks called markers or yardage markers lying flush along the fairways. The numbers and colors indicate yardages to the center of the green: 200 yards (blue), 150 yards (white), and 100 yards (red). On some courses, special trees, shrubbery, or poles are used as markers.

Marked Sprinkler Heads

Many golf courses now use sprinkler heads as yardage markers. Since the heads of most fairway sprinkler systems are spaced about every 30 yards, they provide golfers with a reliable way of finding distance to the green.

I recall a sprinkler head on a particularly long hole at an Idaho course. On it was printed both the yardage and a message, "NO WAY"—a suggestion that even the longest hitter should refrain from attempting to reach the green from that distance.

Military Golf

The term military golf describes when a player in the group hits the ball from one side of the fairway (or the rough bordering it) to the opposite side of the fairway or rough, back to the other side again, and so on. In a way, it's like a march cadence heard in the military: left–right–left–right.

Religious Golf

Religious golf is just like military golf—with the player making a cross here, a cross there, and so on.

Obstruction (Movable or Immovable)

An obstruction is anything artificial (man-made) that has been placed on the course, as opposed to a naturally growing object or something that has been in the same spot since before the course was built, like a boulder. If an obstruction can be easily moved—without requiring much physical effort, without slowing play, and without damaging the course—it is deemed movable. Otherwise, it is considered immovable. In both situations, relief may be granted. Consult your local golf pro or *The Rules of Golf*.

One-Ball Rule

Golf's one-ball rule requires that players use balls of the same brand and compression throughout a round. This eliminates the possibility that a player might gain an advantage from, say, using a hard-cover ball for extra distance when driving from the tees and on long shots, then switching to a soft-cover ball for short shots.

On the Fly

A golf ball is on the fly when its total flight distance is achieved in the air, with little or no roll once it lands.

Out of Bounds

For a ball to be considered out of bounds, it must be completely beyond the playing area. At most courses the playing areas and out of bounds are clearly defined with white stakes.

Players are prohibited from playing a ball that is out of bounds. However, a player can stand out of bounds and hit a ball that is lying on the course.

Pace (of Play)

Pace of play is how quickly a round progresses. Each course has guidelines on how fast groups of two, three, or four golfers should play each hole and an entire round of 18 holes. Each group of players is responsible for keeping pace with the group playing ahead of them.

Out of Position
Playing Through

Golfers are said to be out of position when they are playing more slowly than they should. A group playing behind an out-of-position group may ask the slower players to step aside so that the speedier group can continue without waiting; this is known as playing through.

Call-Up Hole

A call-up hole—always a par 3—offers another way to speed up play. One group—on the green and ready to putt—may call up the group next in line for that hole and stand out of the way while the group tees off. While the group that has just teed off walks or drives to the green, the first group completes their play on the green. Call-up holes don't really save much time, but on a busy course every little bit helps.

Put It in Their Back Pocket

When a slow group seems oblivious to a faster group or has not acknowledged their wish to play through, the faster group may hit balls close to the group ahead to get them to hurry up. When this happens, the faster players are said to put it in the back pocket of the slower ones.

Penalty Stroke

Under *The Rules of Golf*, penalty strokes are assessed. A penalty stroke (in some cases two) is added to the score of any player who breaks a rule.

Play It Where It Lies

A golfer who hits a ball from wherever she finds it without touching the ball or the ground around it is said to play it where it lies.

Provisional Ball

When a ball is either lost or out of bounds—anywhere other than in a water hazard—the player may opt to save time by playing another ball from the same spot. This replacement ball (called a provisional ball) becomes the official ball in play if the original ball can't be found after five minutes of searching.

Pull a String

When a ball lands on the green, then backs up from the spot where it lands, the player who made the shot is said to have pulled the string. If the movement of the ball puts it closer to the hole, so much the better.

Quiet Feet

Quiet feet is a swing style. The player keeps his body still, swinging mostly with his arms.

Range Finder

Range finders are handheld electronic devices equipped with laser or some other technology for measuring the distance from a ball to the target. The golf carts at some resort courses are equipped with range finders. Range finders are not permitted in any play except informal competition.

Reachable Par 5

A par-5 hole that is short enough for a player to reach the green in two strokes (three strokes is G-I-R on a normal par-5 hole) is a reachable par 5. A player has a better-than-average chance of scoring below par on such a hole.

Drivable Par 4
Driving the Green

A par-4 hole that is short enough for a player to reach the green with a tee shot is called a drivable par 4. Making such a shot is called driving the green.

Rough
First Cut of Rough

Rough is any area of a golf course through the green that contains high grass or trees but is considered playable. The term rough is common in golf, but it is not officially recognized in *The Rules of Golf*.

Grass bordering the fairway that has been mown to a height a little taller than that of the fairway grass is called the first cut of rough.

Primary Cut

The primary cut is the predominant height of grass in the rough lining the fairway of each hole. It is kept at this height both to reduce course maintenance costs and to make the rough a bad lie for wayward shots from the tee or fairway.

Rub of the Green

Rub of the green is a golf term that, when used accurately, applies only to a specific situation—when a moving ball touches an object or a person not involved in the play. For example, a player in a tournament whose ball sails into the gallery and bounces off someone is said to be feeling the rub of the green. The phrase is also often used in golf simply to describe bad luck.

Running Ball

A ball that lands and rolls a great distance (say, 25 yards or more) is called a running ball.

Safe Side

Any place along a fairway where there is little or no potential trouble is known as the safe side.

Sand Save

A player who hits into a greenside bunker and still succeeds in making par on the hole has made a sand save.

Second Ball

When an official ruling is needed during play, a golfer may elect to hit a second ball as he awaits the ruling. He plays the second ball from the point of the dispute and continues to play both balls to the finish of the hole. He then gets an official ruling so that he knows which score to count. If he happens to score the same with both balls, he simply records that score and continues play with the original ball.

Short Game

The short game in golf is usually considered to be any shots made from within 100 yards of the hole. Statistically, about 63 percent of the game of golf is played within 100 yards of the hole.

Slam Dunk

A ball that goes into the hole on the fly, disappearing as if by magic, is called a slam dunk. This term is borrowed from basketball.

Spin

Spin is the rotation on a ball caused by the impact of the clubface and the ball. Depending on where and how the clubface strikes the ball, a ball may have sidespin, backspin, and top spin (or forward spin). Golfers learn how to create different kinds of spin to suit different situations.

Staked Tree

A newly planted tree on a golf course that is supported by a pole stuck into the ground is called a staked tree. To protect staked trees, golf has special rules that give a player relief away from the tree without penalty.

Stopped the Bleeding

A golfer who gets a good score on a hole after playing poorly on a series of previous holes is said to have stopped the bleeding. This term is not specific to golf.

Stuffed It
Hit It Stiff

A player who makes a shot that lands close to the hole and stays where it lands is said to have stuffed it or hit it stiff.

Swale

A swale is a low or scooped area of land anywhere on a course that golfers have to hit over, much as they would a ditch.

"Take It Deep"

Once a player is under par for a round, someone might tell him to "take it deep," a way of encouraging him to continue lowering his score from that point to the end of the round.

Take (Obstacle) Out of Play
(Obstacle) Comes into Play

An obstacle or hazard may or may not be reachable in one shot. When it *is* reachable in one shot, the obstacle is said to come into play. For example, a water hazard that is 175 yards from the tee comes into play for anyone who can hit the ball 175 yards. The hazard is not in play for a player who can't hit 175 yards from the tee.

A golfer who takes an obstacle out of play makes a deliberate shot away from the obstacle—and perhaps away from the target itself. The golfer believes that taking one extra stroke at this point is preferable to having to take even more strokes should she attempt to get past the obstacle.

Thread the Needle

A golfer who is in the woods, with only a small space to hit through to get back to the fairway, may feel as if he is trying to put a piece of thread through the eye of a needle.

Through the Fairway

A shot that lands in the fairway and rolls into the rough is said to be through the fairway. This happens more often on dogleg holes and holes with divided fairways.

Divided Fairway

A divided fairway is like a road with a median—and the terrain and level of difficulty are different on the two sides. In some situations, a golfer can choose to play either the right or the left side.

Through the Green

Through the green is an official golf phrase that refers to everything on a golf course except teeing grounds, greens, and hazards.

Throwing Darts

When a golfer can make his approach shots land close to the hole and stay there, he is said to be throwing darts.

"Trees Are 90 Percent Air"

When a golfer is faced with having to get her ball past a tree, she may say to herself, "Trees are 90 percent air"—in the hope that her shot will sail through the leaves and branches of the tree.

Tree Wood

A golfer whose shot hits a tree may hear someone else in his playing group say, "Did you hit your tree wood?"—a pun on "3-wood."

The term is used in another context as well. A player whose only shot appears to be one that will surely hit a tree may be advised to select a tree wood.

Trouble

Trouble is a name for obstacles on a course that may result in penalty strokes for playing into them or near them.

An anecdote: A tourist from a city was visiting a resort-area golf course and overheard a player who'd just finished a round say she'd had "some real trouble on the back nine." The tourist, showing genuine concern, thought the player had been assaulted and wanted to know if she was all right. The tourist was embarrassed—but pleased that the trouble hadn't been of the life-threatening variety.

Trouble Clubs

Some golf clubs are advertised by their manufacturer as trouble clubs—that is, clubs that are able to get players out of bad spots.

Trouble clubs may also refer to clubs that a player relies on for tricky shots that require imagination and a deft touch.

Turn It Over

Turn it over is a phrase used in golf to command the ball to continue to turn over—or roll—once it lands. To make a ball roll over, a golfer must put the right amount of forward spin on the ball when hitting it.

Two- or Three-Club Green

Golfers trying to reach the hole from anywhere off the green must take into consideration the distance to the green plus the distance from the center of the green to the hole. If a player is 100 yards from the center of the green but the pin is 20 yards beyond the green's center, the player must use a club that will hit the ball 20 yards farther than the yardage marker indicates. This would be a two-club green because the golfer needs a club two numbers lower—one for each 10 yards. A three-club green would require three clubs lower in number, and so on.

Professional golfers must also consider the depth of the green because they measure distance to the front of the green and then add paces (yardage) to the hole.

Unplayable Ball

An unplayable ball has been damaged in such a way that its characteristics are changed and it is unfit for play. This includes a ball that is cut, cracked, or out of shape.

Vanilla-Type Game

Golfers who play the game in a rather plain, unspectacular manner are said to have a vanilla-type game. This compliment means they hit a lot of fairways and greens in regulation and score very well. They're just not very emotional or flashy in their style of play.

Worm Burner

A golf ball is a worm burner when it doesn't fly high and—when it lands on the fairway—runs so fast that worms underground will feel the heat as the ball rolls over them.

"When It's Breezy, Just Swing Easy"

Buffeting winds can be difficult to play in. Golfers have a tendency to fight the wind by planting their feet and swinging hard, not realizing that swinging easily is much more effective.

About Winds

There are seven types of wind conditions commonly mentioned on the golf course:

Against the Wind
Into the Wind

When wind is blowing directly into a golfer's face, he is playing against the wind, also called into the wind. For every 10 miles per hour the wind is blowing in your face, you need to use the next-longest (lower-numbered) club to counteract the wind's effects on the ball's flight. For example, the wind is blowing 20 miles per hour and you are playing into the wind. For a shot under normal conditions, you would hit a 7-iron. In this wind, you will need to hit a 5-iron.

Crosswind

A crosswind blows either from left to right or from right to left as a player tries to play toward the green. Any spin the golfer puts on the ball that is in the same direction as the wind will magnify the curve of the ball.

For example, if a right-hander plays a draw into wind blowing from right to left, the wind will cause the ball to curve farther to the left than normal. By the same token, a fade played under the same wind conditions would hold against the wind and not fly as far right.

Downwind
With the Wind

A downwind blows in the same direction as the hole plays, the wind hitting the players' backs when they face the hole. As golfers play toward the green, or with the wind, they may need less club for each shot because the wind helps carry the ball forward—and much farther.

Swirling Wind

A swirling wind is probably the most difficult wind in which to play because it doesn't blow from a constant direction. Instead, its changing direction makes playing conditions unpredictable.

Two-Club Wind (or One- or Three-Club Wind)

When hitting into the wind, for every 10 miles per hour the wind blows, a golfer should select one longer club (lower-numbered) to go the same distance. If the wind is blowing 20 miles per hour, it is known as a two-club wind, 10 miles per hour is a one-club wind, 30 would be a three-club wind, and so on. I've played in a six-club wind, but I don't recommend it.

Congratulations! You're almost home.

Green
Gab

195 Terms Used on and Around the Green

ALL ABOUT GREENS

Putting Green
Green
Putting Surface

Each hole on a course has a closely mown area at the end of the fairway, called the green or putting green, that contains the hole (explained in "Pro Shop Patter"), the putting surface, and the flagstick. There is a green at the end of each hole of play.

Dance Floor

The dance floor is another name for the putting green. Perhaps it got that nickname because people often do a little jig when they sink a difficult putt.

Home

Golfers also refer to the green as home, because that is where they want to be.

Cup
Lip of the Cup

Cup is another term for the hole in the ground on each green, the target a golfer must reach in order to score. The edge of the cup is known as the lip.

Flagstick
Flag

The flagstick is the pole with a banner on top that extends up from the hole of each green. The flagstick stands high enough above the green to help golfers see where to aim. The term flag is used both for where the hole is located on a green and as an abbreviation for flagstick.

Pin

Pin is another term for the flagstick. It is also used interchangeably with hole and cup because they're all in the same place.

Hole Location
Pin Placement

Where a hole is cut into the green is known as the hole location, or pin placement. At most golf courses, the location of the hole is changed almost daily. This is done for two reasons: (1) to prevent wear and tear on the part of the green where the hole is located; and (2) to make the course more challenging, especially for those who play the course frequently.

Pin Sheet

At most major amateur and professional tournaments, players are given a pin sheet, which is a schematic of all the course's greens. The pin sheet shows the distance from the front to the back of each green and the exact pin location. The purpose of the pin sheet is to help players plan their game strategy.

Most courses do not provide pin sheets for everyday play. However, more and more courses now have flag systems to help golfers with pin placements.

Flag System

Flag systems have one color flag for front hole locations, a second color for center placement, and a third for holes at the back of the green. When you play a course for the first time, ask if there is some kind of flag system in place.

Depth of Green
D-O-G
Paces on the Green

Depth of green is another way of indicating the distance from the front to the back of a green. It is also known as D-O-G (spelled out, never as the word DOG).

Hole locations on greens may appear to be closer or farther than they really are, so players may estimate the actual hole location. Some scorecards list the D-O-G, and players can use it along with the flag system to determine distances.

The Fringe
Frog Hair

The area around the edge of the putting surface is commonly called the fringe. If you look at a green, you'll see that the grass on the green's edge is a bit taller than the grass of the green but shorter than the grass just beyond it. Course superintendents mow the grass at different heights to keep the different parts of the course distinct.

I grew up calling this fringe frog hair. Since frogs don't have hair, I'm not sure where the term came from, but one golfer told me that since he was a boy he'd used the phrase "There's only a frog hair of difference" to suggest one thing being almost the same as another. Many credit Bing Crosby with making the term a part of golf vernacular.

The Surround
The Collar

Other terms for the fringe of a green are the surround and the collar. These terms are used more by course superintendents than by players.

The Apron

Some greenkeepers create a larger fringe in front of the green and call it the apron.

Aerated Greens
Plugged Greens

The terms aerated greens and plugged greens refer to greens whose grass has been specially grown using a process that subjects the grass to more air and water. This process involves punching holes in the turf, removing plugs of grass from those holes, then filling them with sand. When greens have been aerated, the sandy patches and the slight depressions on the surface—which result from the holes that have been punched—keep balls from rolling true on the green for about a week.

High Side of the Hole
Pro Side of the Hole
Low Side of the Hole
Amateur Side of the Hole

Although a hole itself may be on even ground, the surrounding area is never perfectly flat. In other words, every hole has a high side and a low side. The high side is also known as the pro side; professional golfers know to putt to the high side of the hole so that the ball has a chance to curve—or break—toward the hole and drop in.

The low side of a hole is also called the amateur side because new golfers have a tendency to underread the curve or break needed to sink a putt from this side of the hole. Golfers often have to remind themselves, especially after failing to make a putt from the low side, that a ball *never* falls up.

Dome-Shaped Greens

A dome-shaped green is a putting surface in the shape of a gently rounded hump. These greens are probably the most difficult to play because a player must try to determine how far his ball will roll down the slopes of the hump.

Buried an Elephant

Referring to a large mound in the middle of a green, a golfer may comment that the course designer buried an elephant in the green.

Turtle-Backed Greens

Like dome-shaped greens, turtle-backed greens have a high, rounded mound in the middle that looks much like the shell of a turtle.

Closely Mown

The grass on greens is closely mown—that is, it is shorter and smoother than grass anywhere else on the course. Owing to climate and other considerations, the length of the grass on greens varies widely from course to course.

Fast Greens
Slow Greens

A green is called fast when even lightly struck balls roll over the green quickly. The speed of a course's greens depends on a number of factors: how short their turf is mowed (shorter is faster), how much slope they have, and how thoroughly and recently they have been watered.

On slow greens, conversely, longer grass, less slope, or excess water forces a golfer to hit the ball harder to reach the hole.

G-I-R
Greens in Regulation

G-I-R is an abbreviation of the phrase "greens in regulation." Every hole on a course has a specified number of strokes that a player needs to reach the green, before taking two putts to score par for the hole. Making this designated number of strokes is known as reaching the green in regulation. Commentators often speak of how many greens a player reaches in regulation, or the number of G-I-R holes she gets.

On a par-3 hole, a player reaches the green in regulation if his tee shot lands on the green. On a par-4 hole, two shots from the tee to the green is considered regulation. And on a par-5 hole, three shots from tee to green is G-I-R.

Holding Greens
Soft Greens

Greens on which a ball lands and rolls hardly at all, coming to rest close to where it lands, are referred to as holding greens or soft greens.

The opposite of fast greens, holding or soft greens seem to embrace the ball, holding it in place.

M-I-A

M-I-A stands for minutes in air—specifically, *after* a ball lands on a hard green and bounces back into the air. Of course, a ball never stays in the air even one minute on this type of rebound, so the term is used by players strictly in fun.

How Much Green to Play With

As a golfer prepares to make any putt or shot onto a green, he has to determine the distance between his ball and the hole in order to figure out what kind of shot to play. In other words, he has to know how much green he has to play with. A pin location toward the back of the green gives the golfer plenty of green to play with, whereas a hole on the near side of the green does not.

In the Face

The term in the face refers to the lie of a ball when it lands in a bunker next to the green. The ball is in the face when it is lodged in the side of the bunker leading up to the green. That is, the ball is staring back into the face of a player positioned across the bunker from the green.

Postage Stamp Green

A very short and very narrow green is called a postage stamp green. The source of this term is Scotland's Royal Troon, whose most famous par-3 hole is named "The Postage Stamp." I have fond memories of the time I played Royal Troon and the birdie I scored on that special hole.

Shaggy Green

A green whose grass has been allowed to grow longer than usual is called a shaggy green. As you might expect, a ball rolls slowly on a shaggy green.

Short Side of the Green

The phrase short side of the green refers to the ball's position in relation to the pin. A ball that is near the hole is on the short side of the green.

Slope of the Green

Every green has a slope that is a result of the natural lay of the land and whatever the course designers felt was needed for efficient drainage. A green's slope is one factor that determines the speed of the putt.

Spike Marks

Tufts of loose, protruding grass on the putting green caused by the shoes of golfers who fail to pick up their feet while walking on the green are called spike marks. Unlike pitch or ball marks, a spike mark may not be repaired until after a player has putted.

Stimpmeter

A Stimpmeter is a handheld device used by tournament officials and members of a course's staff to determine the speed of greens. A rating of 10 to 12 on the Stimpmeter means a green is fast. The lower the number, the slower the putting surface.

Two-Tiered Greens
Three-Tiered Greens

Greens that have two distinct level surfaces are called two-tiered greens. Typically, these tiers are separated by an incline rise of from two to five feet. Some greens have three levels and are called three-tiered.

PLAYING THE GREEN

Putt
A putt is a stroke made on the green, causing a ball to roll and go into or near the hole. Putters are the club of choice for these shots but are not a requirement.

All-Around Good Putt
An all-around good putt is one that circles, or rims, the hole before falling into the cup.

All Over the Pin
A shot that looks as if it's been hit the correct distance and directly in line with the flagstick—whether or not it stops next to the flagstick or actually goes into the hole—is referred to as being all over the pin.

Attending the Flag
Attending the flag is holding the flagstick in the hole while a player prepares to putt. This is done so that the player who is putting can keep the hole location fixed in his mind. As soon as the putt is hit, the person attending the flag removes the flagstick from the hole so that it won't be hit by the ball, a penalty under *The Rules of Golf*.

Balky Putter

A golfer who makes a jerky, uncoordinated putt—seeming to stop in midstroke—might blame his "balky putter" for the mis-hit.

Big Breaker

A big breaker is a putt that makes a wide arc or curve—almost a turn—as it travels along the surface of the green toward the hole.

Bold Putter

A bold putter regularly strikes putts so firmly that the ball travels well beyond the hole—as much as four to five feet—before stopping.

Break

Break is the curve a putted ball makes as it travels toward the hole. The slower the speed of a ball and the steeper the slant of the surface on which it's rolling, the more the ball will break.

Borrow

Borrow is how much curve the golfer *thinks* the ball will make; break is the curve the ball *does* make.

Borrow Too Much
Borrow Too Little

A player who borrows too much hits the ball expecting it to break a lot more than it does. A player borrows too little if the ball curves more than she expects.

Burned the Edge

A putt that has traveled fast toward the hole, then rolled across the outside edge of the hole but not dropped in, is said to have burned the edge.

"Can It!"

Unlike the non-golf expression "Can it!," which is used to tell someone to be quiet, in golf "Can it!" is a remark made to encourage a player to make a putt.

Cellophane on the Hole
Lid on It

When it seems that an invisible barrier is preventing balls from dropping into a hole, the hole is said to have cellophane on it. A hole may also be said to have a lid on it, which means the same thing.

Change Behind the Ball

Change behind the ball refers to the preference among some golfers for marking the position of a ball on the green with a coin (change) rather than with a regular ball marker. Some players think it's good luck to do this, and it's permissible under *The Rules of Golf*.

Closest to the Pin

When several golfers are aiming for the same hole, the player whose ball lands on the putting green nearest the hole is said to be closest to the pin.

K-P

K-P means closest to the pin with bad spelling. K-Ps are usually found only in tournaments, where a special K-P contest may be set up on a par-3 hole. The player whose shot from the tee lands closest to the hole is the winner. K-Ps are many golfers' favorite contest to win. Professional tournaments don't permit K-Ps, but many celebrity tournaments and pro-ams do.

Clutch Putt

A clutch putt is one a player must make in order to stay in his current position—for example, to maintain his lead or take the lead in a game or tournament. Justin Leonard made a spectacular clutch putt in the 1999 Ryder Cup that gave the American team the win.

Cross-Handed
Left Hand Low/Low Left Hand

Normally a right-handed golfer places his right hand lower than his left when putting, just as he would for a full swing. Cross-handed is putting with the left hand lower than the right. Left hand low and low left hand mean the same thing as cross-handed. To describe the same things with respect to left-handers, reverse the hand positions.

Double Break

When a putt curves first in one direction and then in the opposite direction, it is said to exhibit a double break. Most putts break in only one direction.

Dying Putt

A putt that slows down almost to a complete stop as it approaches the hole is called a dying putt. Dying putts rarely make it into the hole. They usually stop just short of the hole, but once in a while they do manage to drop in.

Early Walk

Sometimes a golfer shows confidence in the putt she has just hit by walking toward the hole while the ball is still rolling. Whether or not the ball goes in, this is known as taking an early walk. Tiger Woods is famous for his early walks.

Flag Hunting

A golfer is flag hunting when he aims well and hits a shot from anywhere on the course that winds up very close to the hole.

Get Inside

When a player in a group hits a shot that lands on the green closer to the hole than the ball(s) already there, that player is said to have gotten inside the others.

Don't Give the Cup Away
Give the Cup Away
Playing the Ball Outside the Cup

These phrases have nothing to do with whether or not a putt is successful. They refer only to whether the ball is aimed directly at the hole or away from it.

For example: Two golfers on a team (or a golfer and his caddie) are conferring on how best to hit a putt. If it looks as if the putter is aiming too far off the direct line to the hole, the partner or caddie may say, "Don't give the cup away," meaning the person putting should aim directly at the hole.

When a player prepares to putt and anticipates the ball making a significant break—or curve—the player will intentionally aim either left or right of the hole, giving the cup away. This is also called playing the ball outside the cup.

Dropped a Shot

Dropped a shot refers to scoring on any hole. When a golfer makes a bogey on a hole, she has a score of one over par on that hole, and drops a shot from par.

Another meaning of this term refers to the status between two competing golfers. When a player scores one stroke higher than her opponent on a hole, she has dropped a shot to her opponent.

Lost a Stroke to Par

Lost a stroke to par means the same thing as dropped a shot, and the two terms are used interchangeably.

"Good-Good"

When two players' balls both land on the green very close to the hole, the players might say, "Good-good," suggesting that they will both certainly hole the ball on the first putt.

Sometimes a player will jokingly say, "Good-good" when both balls land on the green but still a long putt from the hole.

Good Leave

A good leave is any shot that puts the ball close to the hole in a spot that leaves the player with a makeable putt.

Good Save

When a golfer makes par on a hole in spite of ragged play from tee to green, he is said to have made a good save.

"Good Weight"

This term may sound like praise for patience, but "good weight" is a comment made to a player who has putted the ball the correct distance to the hole but not quite in the right direction.

Go to School

Frequently two players' balls land on the green so near each other that the players will putt on almost the same exact line to the hole. As always, the player whose ball is farther from the hole putts first. The second player can go to school by watching this putt and seeing how his own putt is likely to break.

"Hit a House"

When a player's putted ball is traveling much faster than the golfer intends, he may yell, "Hit a house!" This is a wish that the ball hit something—anything—to slow it down. The exhortation also allows a player to vent frustration over a wayward putt.

Hole Can Jump Up and Bite You

Sometimes a particular pin location looks deceptively easy to hit from a player's ball location and he doesn't put a lot of attention into lining up the putt—only to find that he needs one or two (or even three) additional putts to get the ball into the hole. The result is often a score on the hole that is much higher than anticipated. When this happens, a player may say that the hole can jump up and bite you.

Hole High
Pin High

You are said to have hit the ball hole high or pin high if, from the vantage point of your shot, you land the ball anywhere even with the hole. This can be on either side—left or right. If the ball lands in front of or behind the hole, you have hit it either short or long.

Home in Two (or Three or Four)

When a player is able to get his ball onto the green in two strokes (or three or four strokes, etc.), it is known as getting home in two (or three or four, etc.).

Inside Right
Inside Left

Inside right and inside left refer to where a golfer should aim a putt so that it will go into the hole. Inside right means the golfer should aim just to the right of the hole's center, assuming that it has to curve slightly to the left to drop in. Inside left is just the opposite.

Jerky Putter

Some golfers are known to have a jerky putter because of their nonrhythmic, unsmooth putting style.

Yips

Golfers who normally have a smooth putting stroke may—because of nerves or pressure to perform—temporarily have the yips, a shaky, jerky, or uncontrolled putting stroke.

GOLF A to Z

Knee-Knocker

A knee-knocker is a short, normally easy putt that is made difficult by circumstance—such as the player's score. Under this kind of pressure, the golfer's knees may knock, either literally or figuratively, and she may not be able to sink the putt.

Lag Putt

A lag putt is a setup shot that ensures that the next putt will be an easy, short one into the hole. For example, a golfer may be faced with a very long putt of, say, 25 feet or more. Rather than try to hole the putt, it is better to just attempt a lag putt—that is, get the ball as close to the hole as possible and try to leave a makeable second putt.

Great Lag

A successful lag putt—one where the ball stops two feet or less from the hole—is called a great lag. A great lag is the same as a good leave.

Lights-Out Putting

Lights-out putting is part of a great day on the golf course. The golfer just can't seem to miss a putt—they all seem to go into the hole.

Line of Putt

The line of putt is the actual direction the ball goes once it's been hit.

Line Up the Putt

Golfers line up the putt by studying the surface of the green and the distance from the ball to the hole in order to determine the direction to hit the putt and how much force to use when striking the ball.

Lipped Out

When a putt rolls to the edge of the hole and starts to drop in, then seems to be spit back out by the cup and rolls away, it is said to have lipped out.

Makeable Putt

A makeable putt is one that the golfer appears to have a better-than-average chance of sinking. Of course, this phrase is used to describe the shot *before* the putt is made.

Never Up, Never In

Never up, never in is an old golf saying used to describe a shot (usually a putt) that is not hit with enough force to reach the hole. In other words, a ball that is not hit *up* to the hole will never have a chance to go *in* the hole.

"Nice Putt, Alice"

When a golfer hits a putt that winds up way short of the hole, he or his partner may comment, "Nice putt, Alice." Whoever the historical Alice was never hit the ball hard enough to reach the hole. This comment is made to male and female golfers alike.

While playing at a country club in Hong Kong, I received a key chain as a gift. On it was a button that triggered an electronic recorded message: "Nice putt, Alice."

No-Brainer

You'd think a no-brainer is a short, easy putt, but it's not. Rather, it is a long putt that miraculously goes into the hole—in many cases, a shot that would otherwise be called a lag putt.

Pace (of Putt)

Not to be confused with the steps you take to measure a green, the speed with which a golf ball rolls after being struck by a putter is its pace. This term has become increasingly popular among television commentators in several different sports.

Plumb Bob

Some players line up their putts using their putter as a guide. This is done by holding the putter at eye level by the top of its shaft and at arm's length, then visually lining up the ball and the hole along the imaginary vector extending out from the putter. Called a plumb bob, this is one way golfers try to determine how a putt will break.

Putt That Runs Away from You

A ball putted on either a downhill slope or with the grain of the grass gains speed as it travels. This is known as a putt that runs away from you.

Putt Through the Break

Normally a putt breaks—or curves—as it slows down, hopefully when it's close to the hole. However, when a putt is going too fast to break until after it has passed the hole, it has been putt through the break.

Reading Greens

Reading greens is the process of figuring out how the physical properties of a green will affect a putt. Typically, a golfer considers factors such as how much break a putt might make; whether the putt will be hit sidehill, uphill, or downhill; whether the stroke will be with or against the grain; and the speed with which the putt should be struck because of the distance it needs to travel.

Underread Greens
Overread Greens

A golfer at times underreads a green—meaning that she thinks the ball will break less than it does. Or a player may overread a green—meaning that she estimates the ball will break more than it does.

Searching for Loose Change

A TV commentator once said of a golfer who was preparing to mark his ball that the player was searching for loose change. By this he meant that the golfer didn't have—or didn't want to use—a regular marker and was about to use a coin instead. It is common (and permissible) to use a coin as a ball marker.

Shoes Have Gone Out of Style

A golfer who has to wait for the others in his group to shoot before he can putt may comment that so much time has elapsed since his last shot that his shoes have gone out of style.

Short-Side Hit

An approach shot that lands near the pin (on the pin side of the green) but not on the green itself is called a short-side hit. From this spot, the next shot is difficult because there isn't much putting surface between the ball and the hole. Nor is there much room for error—the shot must be precise or it may travel far past the hole.

Sidesaddle Putting

In the normal style of putting, the golfer stands sideways to the hole, holds the putter in front of him, and swings across the front of his body. In sidesaddle putting, the golfer faces the hole and holds the putter next to his body, then swings the putter forward—along the side of his body—and toward the hole.

"Sink It"

"Sink it" is a term that one player uses to encourage another to make a putt.

Slider

A slider is a sidehill, downhill putt. Typically, it is very difficult to execute because the ball tends to break quickly and sharply, moving away from the hole as it rolls.

Spanked It

When a player slaps a putt really hard, she has spanked it. This means the player made a jab at the ball rather than a smooth, rhythmic stroke through the ball.

Speed Putt

A speed putt is a fast putt that breaks a lot as it travels toward the hole. If it's executed correctly, its pace and line will allow it to break just enough to go into the hole.

Spot Putt

A golfer makes a spot putt when he selects a particular point on the green as a target along the break of the putt much closer than the hole. This can be a blade of grass or a small bump, for example. The player hopes that the putt will cross this more easily reachable spot and go into the hole.

Stepping in Someone's Line

Players frequently walk around the perimeter of the green behind their golf balls and the marks of all the other players in the group. Some players may even be seen taking very large strides, as if attempting to step over something. These players are trying to avoid stepping in another golfer's putting line.

Golf etiquette dictates that you *never* step in someone's line. Failure to observe this rule may result in footprints that leave temporary depressions in the turf and affect the roll of a ball.

Stony

A shot that is hit so close to the hole that it sets up an easy putt is sometimes called a stony—that is, it has landed just a stone's throw from the hole.

Stuck It

A player whose shot has landed close to the hole and barely rolled is said to have stuck it.

Stymies

Until 1951, there was a rule in golf—called stymies—that was applied whenever two putts wound up within six inches of each other. The player whose ball was closer to the pin was not allowed to place a ball mark or move the ball; the player farther from the hole had to either chip over his opponent's ball (if it was in the way) or go around it.

Sucker Pin Placement

A sucker pin placement is one that looks easy to hit but actually involves a lot of risk. For example, players may be tempted to try for a pin located near a hazard because the pin appears to be easily reachable—only to wind up in the hazard.

Sword Fight

Sometimes a golfer simply misses an easy putt, then attempts a tap-in that goes past the hole. So she hits the ball without lining it up and misses the hole again.

Several slashing mis-hits later, this has become a one-person sword fight.

Tester

A tester is a short but difficult putt that tests the golfer's ability. If successfully made, the golfer has passed the test.

Texas Wedge

A Texas wedge is a putter used an exceptionally long distance from off the green. The term originated in Texas, which is known for its strong winds—and the ostensible purpose of the shot is to keep the ball on the ground so that the wind won't have any effect on it.

Three-Jacked It

A golfer who takes three putts to sink a ball is said to have three-jacked the hole. Obviously, the term does not refer to Jack Nicklaus.

White-Knuckler

Similar to a knee-knocker, a white-knuckler is a putt that would be easy were it not for the fear brought on by other considerations—such as tournament standings or friendly wagering. The term refers to what happens when a player clutches his putter so hard that his knuckles turn white.

With the Grain

With the grain means the putt is hit in the same direction the grass grows and lies. Putts made with the grain roll faster than putts made against the grain. If the grass appears to have a sheen, you are putting with the grain.

Wrong Side of the Hole

A ball that settles in a spot on the green from which it is almost impossible to sink a putt has landed on the wrong side of the hole. The ball may be left uphill from the hole, or on a sidehill slope, or far away from the hole, or tucked near the fringe of the green. Wrong side of the hole is the opposite of a good leave.

"You Can Have the Pin"

When a player is about to attempt a shot onto the green from off the green, a member of his group may say, "You can have the pin." This means that the shooter has permission from his playing partners to leave the flagstick in the hole while he shoots and he will not be penalized if his golf ball hits the flagstick.

A true story: As he was preparing to make a pitch shot to the green, a new golfer was told that he could have the pin. The player immediately dropped his club, walked across the green to the hole, grabbed the flagstick, walked back to his cart, and put the flagstick in his golf bag.

He thought he had been given the flag as a gift.

"You're Away"

"You're away" is an expression used on the green to help players determine the order in which they will shoot. The player whose ball lies farthest—or away—from the hole always shoots first. This is part of the "honors" system practiced on the green and elsewhere.

"You're Still Away"
U-S-A

"You're still away" is used when a player has honors on successive putts. It is not a term of praise because it means the player to whom it is addressed wasn't successful on his last putt. The phrase is sometimes abbreviated "U-S-A."

WAYS TO SCORE

Albatross
Double Eagle

An albatross is the same as a double eagle—a score of three under par on any hole. A golfer who scores an albatross, or a double eagle, takes only two strokes to complete a par-5 hole or one stroke for a par-4. These names are in keeping with the other ornithological terms for scores under par—birdie (one under) and eagle (two under).

A famous albatross was made by Gene Sarazen, who passed away in 1999 at the age of 97. This "shot heard 'round the world" was his second shot that went into the hole on the par-5 15th hole in the 1935 Masters Tournament in Augusta, Georgia, which allowed him to tie

Craig Wood for the tournament lead. Sarazen won the next day in a 36-hole play-off.

Answered It
When one golfer makes a putt for a given score in match-play competition, her opponent may then have to make a putt in order to tie the hole. If the second player makes this critical putt, she is said to have answered it.

Ball Holed
A ball is officially holed when it comes to rest inside the hole and is completely below the top edge of the hole.

Birdie
Bird
A birdie, sometimes called a bird, is a score of one under par on any hole.

Bogey
A bogey is a score of one over par on any hole. It's every golfer's goal to score a birdie; it's every golfer's fear to score a bogey.

Double Bogey
Double
Buzzard
A double bogey is a score of two strokes over par on any hole. It also goes by the names double and buzzard.

Bold Stroke

A putt that is hit too firmly but somehow goes into the hole is called a bold stroke.

Canned It

A golfer has canned it when he hits a hard putt that miraculously goes into the hole.

Chip In/Chipped In

A golfer who hits a short shot from off the green that goes into the hole has chipped in, or has made a chip-in.

No Putt

If a golfer uses a putter from off the green, it is not counted as a putt—it is a no putt.

Concede a Putt

A player who lets his opponent pick up his ball rather than make him hit a very short putt is said to have conceded the putt. Only in match play is a player allowed to concede a putt.

Of course, the player to whom the putt is conceded must add one stroke to his score, just as he would if he had actually putted the ball into the hole.

Deuce

Deuce is a score of two on any hole; a player who scores a deuce needed only two strokes to hole the ball. On a par-3 hole, a deuce is a birdie. On a par-5 hole, it is a double eagle.

Drained a Putt
Drilled It

Drained a putt and drilled it are two ways golfers describe having made a putt despite hitting the ball hard.

Dropped In

A golf ball is said to have dropped in when it gently rolled into the hole.

Eagle

An eagle is a score of two under par on any hole. On a par-3 hole, an eagle is the same as an ace.

Even Par

A player at even par has hit the precise number of strokes the course has designated as par for that point in the round. A golfer can be at even par at the end of one hole, after several holes, or at the end of a round of play.

Level Par

Level par is the British way of saying even par.

Gimme
"Pick It Up"

A gimme is a shot that lands close enough to the hole that there's virtually no way the ball will miss the hole on the next putt. Other players in the group may tell the player with the gimme to "Pick it up." This is the same as conceding a putt but is only allowed in friendly games. If you're told to "Pick it up," don't forget to add a stroke to your score.

Hat Trick

In golf, a hat trick is making birdies on three consecutive holes in a single round. The term was probably borrowed from ice hockey, where it is used to refer to scoring three goals in the same game.

Holed It

A player who makes a shot that goes into the cup is said to have holed it.

Holed Out

A golfer has holed out when she has completed a hole of play.

H-I-O
Hole-in-One

H-I-O is the abbreviation for hole-in-one—hitting a ball from the tee into the hole with one stroke.

Scoring an H-I-O is a cause for celebration, and many golfers who accomplish the feat proudly display a commemorative trophy complete with the ball used. A hole-in-one must be witnessed and the scorecard signed by those witnesses to be officially recognized.

Hole Swallowed It
When a putt travels quickly toward the cup and goes in, almost as if the hole reached out for the ball, it is said that the hole swallowed it.

Horseshoe the Hole
A putted ball horseshoes the hole when it circles the cup's edge but, instead of dropping in, rolls back onto the putting surface in the direction from which it was hit.

In the Back Door
A ball is said to go in the back door when it rolls past the front of the cup, then curves and falls into the hole from behind.

In the Side Door
A ball that goes into the hole from either the right or the left side, rather than into the center of the cup on a straight-line approach from the putter, is said to have gone in the side door.

In the Heart
A shot that goes into the hole's dead center—rather than from either side or the back—is said to be in the heart.

In the Hole
In the Jar

Any ball, either driven or putted, that winds up in the cup is said to be in the hole or in the jar. Jar is a nickname for the hole.

In the Jaws
In the Throat

In the jaws and in the throat are other ways of describing a ball that has gone into the hole. As with the hole swallowed it, these phrases are used when the ball has traveled so quickly that it seems to have been caught by the mouth of the cup.

Opened the Door
Shut the Door

A tournament leader who misses a putt that gives other players a chance to tie for the lead or take the lead outright is said to have opened the door for his opponents. Conversely, a player who makes such a putt is said to have shut the door on his opponents.

Scoring an "Other"

TV commentators used to call a score of triple bogey or worse an "other" as a way of helping the golfer save face. However, these days commentators increasingly seem to enjoy reporting when a professional golfer makes a high score, and the term is rarely heard anymore, at least in the United States.

Quad

Quad is a shorthand way of saying quadruple bogey—for example, a score of eight on a par-4 hole.

Scoring Opportunity

A golfer is said to have a scoring opportunity when he has hit a shot so well that he is almost assured of making a birdie or an eagle—to score under par on that hole—and thus improve (or lower) his overall score.

Seagoer

A long putt—say, from one end of a green to the other—that goes in the hole is called a seagoer, perhaps because it seems to have traveled the seven seas before dropping in.

Snake

A weaving, long (40 feet or more) putt that goes into the hole is called a snake.

Steal One

A player steals one when she manages to score under par on a hole after making poor shots.

360-Degree Putt
Toilet Flusher

A 360-degree putt is one that goes completely around the hole before dropping in. A toilet flusher is a putt that swirls around inside the hole.

Takes Advantage of the Shot

A player who lands a shot close to the hole and then sinks the next putt is said to have taken advantage of the first shot.

Tap-In

A tap-in is a putt, made only a few inches from the hole, that seems almost impossible to miss.

10-Second Rule

The 10-second rule comes into play when a putt comes to rest at the edge of the hole. The player may wait 10 seconds for the putt to drop in, then must make another stroke for a tap-in. Golfers have used all kinds of tricks to get balls to drop in within the allotted 10 seconds: jumping up and down, pounding their putters on the ground, and placing their bodies between the sun and the ball to create a shadow that will make the grass blades lie down and the ball fall in. Of these, only the shadow method is permitted.

Tracking Putt

A putt that is hit as if it were a train running on a railroad track—straight to the hole—is called a tracking putt. Once the ball is hit, it seems there is nothing it can do but go in—that is, it is on just the right track with just the right speed.

Triple

Triple is a nickname for triple bogey, a score of three strokes over par on a single hole.

Up and Down

Up and down is a commonly heard phrase that refers to a situation where a player fails to reach the green in regulation but then makes an approach shot *up* on the green and one-putts the ball *down* into the hole. For most statistics in professional tournaments, up and downs count only on those holes when a player scores par or lower.

Up and In

Up and in means the same thing as up and down, but it isn't used quite as often.

Within the Leather

Within the leather is a phrase that refers to an informal and unofficial way of determining if a player's ball is close enough to the hole to offer the player a gimme or concede the putt.

A ball is within the leather if it is not farther away from the hole than the shaft of the player's putter when the club is laid on the ground, its head in the hole and its grip end pointing toward the ball. If the ball is even with the putter's grip or farther, it is not within the leather.

This phrase has been around a long time—ever since grips were made of leather.

And now the 19th hole awaits you.

Clubhouse
Chatter

172
TERMS THAT MIGHT BE DISCUSSED AT THE 19TH HOLE OR BETWEEN ROUNDS

Because so many golf courses have 18 holes, the 19th hole has become synonymous with clubhouse as the place to gather after completing a round of golf. The 19th hole usually offers beverages, a big-screen TV showing some golf event, and a companionable atmosphere for people to celebrate, review their game, and talk about any golf topic they wish.

PRO GOLF TOPICS AND TOURNAMENTS

Tour Player
Tours
Mini-Tours
A tour player is one who makes a living playing in golf competitions for prize money. The best-known tours in the United States are the PGA, the LPGA, and the Senior Tours. Lesser known are the mini-tours, such as Buy.com and the Futures Tour, which are the equivalent of golf's minor leagues.

Inside the Ropes
During most professional tournaments and many large amateur events, galleries are kept behind ropes—usually yellow ones—that line sides of fairways and areas around tees and greens. Players hope to keep their play inside the ropes most of the time.

The Field
The field is a common term that refers to both the number and the names of the players participating in a tournament.

Stipulated Round
A stipulated round is the number of holes a golfer will officially play and score in a competitive event—typically 18 holes in the numerical order. However, a stipulated round may officially be declared to be fewer than 18 holes.

Marker (the Person)

A marker is someone who keeps score for one or more competitors in a stroke-play tournament. A marker may or may not be playing in the tournament, but he walks along with the players.

Posting a Score

In both professional and amateur tournaments, each player must sign and turn in a correct scorecard at the end of a round. This is called posting a score. Scores are then displayed on a scoreboard inside or outside the clubhouse, which allows spectators and players to see for themselves how the tournament is progressing.

Attest

Attest refers to a player's signature confirming that another player's hole-by-hole score for a round is correct. Since two signatures are required to make a scorecard official, there are two spaces on a scorecard for signatures. One is labeled "scorer" and the other "attest." Ultimately, a player is responsible for the accuracy of his own hole-by-hole score but not for the correct total for the round of play.

During a tournament, players and attesters check scores, sign scorecards, and turn them in for official posting. The same process is used by a witness to an amateur golfer's hole-in-one.

Leader Board

The scores of players in a tournament are posted on what is called the leader board. All players in a tournament are listed on the this board, not just the leaders.

Black Numbers
In the Black

Par or higher on any hole is a score in the black numbers. When scores are posted on a tournament leader board, these numbers are printed in black. This is also known as being in the black.

Red Numbers
In the Red

Scores under par on a hole are printed in red numbers on the leader board. Golfers shooting in the red have an overall score lower than par. Their total scores continue to be printed in red as long as they stay under par. Unlike the financial world, where the goal is to be "in the black," the goal in golf is to be "in the red."

Caveman

When a professional golfer makes a score in the 90's, it's called scoring a caveman. There are several rumors about the origin of this term. One is that cavemen were in the dark, and thus a golfer scoring in the 90's is in the dark as well. Another is that someone with a high score may feel as if his clubs resemble those of a caveman, which of course are unsuitable for hitting a golf ball.

Snowman

A snowman is a score of eight on a single hole. This term will be readily understood by anyone who has ever seen a snowman made with two large balls of snow, just like the number 8.

Hockey Sticks

A total score of 77 in an 18-hole round of golf is called hockey sticks.

(Number) of Strokes Up
Lost a Stroke to the Field

During a tournament, you may hear a commentator say that a certain player is so many strokes up. If a player is ahead by five strokes, for example, an announcer may say that the player is five strokes up. Then, if the player scores higher on a hole, the announcer may say that she is now only four strokes up. When this happens, it means that the player has lost a stroke to the field.

Left Shots Out There
Left Them Out There

A golfer may lament the missed opportunities to lower his score (with birdies or eagles, for example) during a just-completed round of play. He may complain that he "left shots out there" or "left them out there"—meaning that he didn't bring those good shots into the clubhouse on his scorecard.

(Number) Out
(Number) Off
(Number) Back

When a tournament lasts more than one round, the scores of all participating players are reported by comparing them to the leader's score. For example, a commentator may say that a player is "five out" or "five off" or "five back." This means that the player is behind the leader by five strokes.

Moving Day
Move Up the Leader Board

Moving day is the third day of a four-day tournament, when the players who have made the cut try to shoot their lowest scores to improve their standings to move up the leader board. Of course, players always try to move up the leader board.

Leader in the Clubhouse
(In the) Driver's Seat

The person with the lowest total score of those who have completed the current round(s) of play is the leader in the clubhouse. A player is said to be in the driver's seat when he has a lead in a tournament of two or more strokes, because it seems he's in control of play.

In the Chase

Any player in contention to win a tournament is said to be in the chase. Several different players may be in contention at different times throughout the course of play.

(Number) in the House

When a player in a tournament has completed a single round with a score of—let's say 67, because it's a very nice score—other players in the clubhouse may say, "There's a 67 in the house." This also means that 67 is the lowest score of the current round, but it does not necessarily mean that the golfer who has scored 67 is the leader in the tournament.

Logjam at the Top of the Leader Board

There is a logjam at the top of the leader board when two or more competitors in a tournament have the same score or are within no more than three strokes of each other.

The Cut

In many amateur tournaments and almost all professional ones, the field of players is cut to a specific number after the first rounds (usually two) have been played. To make the cut, a player has to have shot no higher than a predetermined score.

On the Bubble

A competitor is on the bubble when she is at or within one stroke of the projected cut score. If the player's final score is higher than the cut score, her bubble has burst and she's going home.

Made the Cut

When a golfer's score is at or below the cut score, he has made the cut and can continue competing in the tournament.

Play-Off

When two (or more) players are tied for the best total score at the end of the final round of a tournament, the winner is determined by a play-off. In one type of play-off, the golfers play a specific number of holes (from one to four), and the player with the lowest overall score wins.

Some play-offs are contested over an entire 18-hole round. If there is still a tie at the end of the 18 holes, the remaining players go into a sudden death play-off.

Sudden Death Play-Off

Sudden death is a type of play-off in which play continues hole by hole until one golfer's score is the lowest on a single hole of play.

Both Hands on the Cup

Both hands on the cup means a player has won a tournament and is able to hold the trophy up—presumably with both hands.

One Hand on the Cup

One hand on the cup means a player either had the lead or was very close to being in the lead toward the end of a tournament but couldn't quite hold on to finish in first place.

Silly Season

When the official professional golf season ends, the silly season begins. The silly season encompasses a series of special tournaments in different formats, including match play, challenges among members of the three major tours (where players from one tour challenge players from another), charity events, and made-for-TV competitions.

Money List

Professional golfers are ranked according to tournament wins and money earned; the earnings ranking is called the money list. However, events and money won during the silly season are not official, and the earnings from those events are not included on the money list.

On the Bag

The caddie for a particular professional golfer is said to be on the bag. For instance, "Fluff" Cowan was on the bag for Peter Jacobsen for several years, then for Tiger Woods at the beginning of Tiger's professional career.

Bib

The over-the-head vest worn by a caddie is called a bib. Most bibs have side ties and bear the name of the player whose clubs the caddie carries. Bibs are worn by the caddies in all professional tournaments and those in some amateur ones as well.

Yardage Book

Yardage books, which are carried by most professional and many amateur golfers, list the exact yardages from tees to greens on a particular course and thus help players plan course strategy and club selection for more effective course management. A course's yardage book also has a schematic drawing of each hole, with landmarks and pertinent yardage information to and from various points along the hole, including the width and depth of the green.

Some golfers keep yardage books on every course they've played. This allows the golfer to play a course again without having to remeasure.

Exempt Player

A player on a professional tour who earns enough money in a given season to rank among the top players on the money list becomes an exempt player for the next season—which means she can enter any tournament without having to play in qualifying rounds. To remain exempt, a player must finish the season in the top 125. Exempt players do not have to go through a new qualifying school.

Nonexempt Player

A nonexempt player on a professional tour may enter a tournament only if the field is not already filled with exempt players. Nonexempt players are ranked at the end of qualifying school to determine the order in which they will be invited into the field of any tournament with available spots for nonexempt players.

Sponsor Exemption

Sometimes a company (or individual) providing financial sponsorship for a tournament designates a player to compete regardless of the player's rank. If the player agrees to play, she enters the tournament as a sponsor exemption.

Q School
Qualifying School

Q school stands for "qualifying school," which is a series of tournaments golfers enter to become eligible to play on the professional tours.

The LPGA, the PGA, and the Senior Tours all have yearly regional tournaments. The top players in these regionals go on to national Q school tournaments. As many as 50 of the top scorers at that Q school become exempt for any event on their respective tours.

Rabbit Qualifying

Rabbit qualifying is the result of a mini-tournament held before an official tournament to help nonexempt golfers qualify for that tournament. Typically, one to four players with the lowest scores in the rabbit qualifying tournament are allowed to play in the official tournament.

Gallery
Outside Agency

People watching a tournament in person are called the gallery. Anyone present at a tournament but not playing in a match is known as an outside agency. The most common (and largest) outside agency at a professional tournament is the gallery, and the rules that apply to outside agencies differ from those for players.

Committee

Committee refers to the specific group of individuals in charge of a golf event. Every course has an oversight committee, even if there is no competitive event taking place at the course.

Decisions on the Rules of Golf
The Rules of Golf
Decisions Book

The *Decisions on the Rules of Golf*, known as the Decisions Book, is the thick companion to *The Rules of Golf*. The Decisions Book is a collection of interpretations of golf rules made by rules officials. These decisions help resolve rules problems arising from the lack of uniformity in golf course design, weather conditions, and so on.

The Majors

Both the men's and the women's U.S. professional tours play four tournaments every year called majors. On the men's tour, the majors are the U.S. Open, the British Open, the PGA Championship, and the Masters Tournament. The women's majors are the U.S. Women's Open, the Women's British Open, the LPGA Championship, and the Nabisco Championship (formerly known as the Dinah Shore).

Amen Corner

Amen corner is the nickname for holes 11, 12, and 13 at Augusta National Golf Club, where the Masters is played. These three holes, the most difficult of the entire course, have helped to determine the results of many a Masters Tournament. The game's lore has it that golfers who play these three holes well say, "Amen" with a smile and that those who play the holes poorly say, "Amen and good-bye"—referring to their chances of winning the tournament.

Grand Slam

Winning all four majors in the same calendar year constitutes a grand slam.

Career Grand Slam

When a golfer wins all four majors in one lifetime, she is known as having won a career grand slam.

Tiger Slam

Tiger slam refers to winning all four majors in succession, although not in the same season. It is named after Tiger Woods, the first person to do it.

Stats

Stats (short for statistics) are kept on each golfer's performance during the season and over the course of his career. As in other major sports, stats are closely watched by the players themselves; people who work with them; the staff of the PGA, LPGA, and Senior Tours; members of the media; and fans. The following are some of the stats recorded in a tournament:

> putts per round
> percentage of greens in regulation
> percentage of driving accuracy
> percentage of sand saves
> driving distance
> score totals for that tournament and scoring
> average

Bounce-Back Stat

Bounce-back is an official statistic, recorded for most professionals, that tells the percentage of time a player is over par on a hole, then under par on the following hole in the same round of play.

Scoring Average

A professional golfer's scoring average is his total strokes for the year divided by the number of 18-hole rounds played in competition. On most courses played by professionals, par is 72. However, some courses built in recent years have pars of 70 or 71. This discrepancy makes computing a player's annual scoring average difficult and makes an adjustment necessary.

Par Breaker

The player on the professional tour who is under par for the greatest percentage of time, regardless of the number of holes played, is known as that tour's par breaker.

Driving Distance

A player's driving distance is the statistical average length of two drives from two specific tees in a professional competition. The drives of all the players in that tournament are measured from these two tees for individual length of drive and averages. These statistics are then compiled throughout the regular season.

Referee

The referee is the person in charge of making decisions when rules are breached during competition. A referee cannot play in any competition that he is officiating.

Observer
An observer is a referee's assistant, whose official job is to report any possible rules violations to the referee.

Vardon Trophy
The player on the PGA Tour with the lowest scoring average for an entire season is given the Vardon Trophy.

Vare Trophy
The LPGA Tour player with the lowest scoring average for the entire season receives the Vare Trophy.

P-A-T
Player Ability Test
P-A-T stands for "player ability test." This is one of the tests that all aspiring club professionals must pass in order to be accepted into the LPGA or the PGA. Golfers trying to become members of either organization must shoot a specific target score—or lower—in a sanctioned tournament held for this purpose to pass the P-A-T.

Pro-Ams
Pay to Play
Pro-ams are tournaments that team a professional player with one or more amateurs in different game formats. The entry fee for amateur golfers is often fairly steep—because part of the money raised in these tournaments is donated to charity. Many amateurs enter these tournaments because, in addition to helping to raise money for

charity, the amateurs get a thrill playing alongside a professional.

Skins Game, Professional
Carryovers
Skinless

Held every Thanksgiving weekend, the Skins Game is a two-day made-for-TV event played for high stakes. Four professionals play 18 holes for skins, which represent money. The prize money per skin increases as holes are played.

When there is a tie for low score on a hole, the prize money or skins total becomes a carryover—that is, it is added to the money or skins being played for on the next hole. A player wins a skin (or skins) when he alone has the lowest score on a hole. A player who wins no skins during the competition is said to be skinless. The winner of the Skins Game is the player who has earned the most money at the end of the competition.

The format changed in 2001: The player who won a hole was not entitled to his skin (the money from that hole as well as any carryover money from previously tied holes) unless he validated the skin by winning or tying the next hole. The jury is still out on how successful this new format is.

Ryder Cup

The Ryder Cup is a famous biennial match-play (unlike the stroke-play format played in professional tour events) competition between the top professional golfers from the United States and Europe. The format is four alternate-shot matches and four best-ball matches on each of the first two days, and twelve 18-hole singles matches on the third day.

The victor in each match receives 1 point. If any match ends in a tie, half a point is given to each side. There is a total of 28 points possible over the three days. The team that wins at least 14½ points wins the Ryder Cup. If the event ends in a tie, the previous winning team retains the Ryder Cup. There is no tie-breaker.

There are other tournaments that feature players from the United States and Europe competing against each other, but these events do not receive the recognition that the Ryder Cup enjoys. They include the Solheim Cup for professional women golfers, the Curtis Cup for amateur women, and the Walker Cup for amateur men.

AMATEUR TOURNAMENTS AND GAMES GOLFERS PLAY

There are many kinds of golf games, and many of these games have a number of variations. In addition to the following games, you can find games listed in *Tee Talk* and other books and publications on the subject. If you enjoy friendly competition, try them all.

Just remember to decide before play begins whether you are using *gross* scores or *net* scores.

Aggregate

Aggregate is a game in which groups of two, three, or four golfers play in teams. All the scores of the players in one group are added together for a single team score. The group with the lowest score is the winner.

Alternate Shot
Scotch Ball
Foursome (the Game)
Straight Scotch

Alternate shot is a game in which two golfers form a team playing one ball, with the players taking alternate shots and only one score being recorded for the team. This game is also known as scotch ball and foursome.

A variation on alternate shot: the player who holes out on the previous hole does not tee off on the next hole. This version of alternate shot is sometimes called straight scotch.

Some golfers play a variation of alternate shot in which one member of the team tees off on odd-numbered holes and the other member of the team tees off on even-numbered holes. This is the format used in Ryder Cup foursome matches.

Barky
Woody

When a player's ball hits a tree somewhere along the fairway and the player still manages to make par—or lower—on that hole, he is said to have made a barky or woody. Named for the parts of a tree, this golfing feat is usually played only in friendly competition for small monetary prizes.

Sandy

When a player hits a ball into a bunker (the sand) and still manages to make a score of par—or less—on that hole, he is said to have made a sandy. Some golfers have special awards for players in their group who make a sandy.

Double Sandy

If you land in two bunkers on the same hole and still make a score of par or less, you get a double sandy—the prize for which is usually double that of a regular sandy.

Baseball

Baseball is a golf game in which three or more people make up a team. They bat—or shoot—in the same order throughout their 9- or 18-hole round of play. On a three-person team, member one hits the tee shot, member two hits the next shot, member three hits the third shot, member one hits the fourth shot, and so on, with only one score recorded for the team on each hole.

Baseball is a great game for new golfers, because players hit only every third or fourth shot, depending on how many players make up the team. This eliminates the pressure of playing an entire round on one's own.

Best Ball
Better Ball

In best ball, the lowest score among the three or four players who make up a team is recorded as the team's score for each hole. The fun thing about best ball is that everyone on the team is encouraged by other members of the team to play well; it doesn't matter which individual player scores lowest because it's the team with the best score at the end of the round that wins. Better ball is the same game but with two-member teams.

Calcutta

Calcutta is a game in which all the teams playing in a tournament are auctioned off—and sold—before the tournament. The auction is open only to the teams in the field of play, and teams are purchased by themselves or by other teams. When a team buys another team, the buyer receives any prizes earned in tournament play by the team that was purchased. However, when a team is sold (for example, for $500), the sold team can buy back their right to keep half of their potential winnings by paying their purchaser one-half of their purchase price (in this example, $250). If a team is sold to themselves, they of course get to keep all their potential winnings.

Callaway System

The Callaway system is a way of determining net-score prizes in a tournament when none of the players have an established handicap. The Callaway system uses a chart to convert each golfer's score to a net score so that play-ers' net scores can be ranked to determine a winner(s).

Chapman

Chapman is a partnership game in which both partners tee off on the first hole, then player A hits player B's sec-ond shot and player B hits player A's second shot. At this point, the game changes. On the third shot, the partners select the better ball, and the ball of the player whose shot is selected is hit by the player whose shot is not selected.

Once the third shot has been hit, the remaining shots are played exactly like scotch ball, using the ball that was selected at the third shot. At the next tee, both partners tee off and the process begins again.

Cross-Country

Cross-country is a game that effectively redesigns the way a course is normally played. On every hole, players hit from the tee of one hole to the green of an entirely dif-ferent hole.

Warning: This format can be used only with the per-mission of the golf course. Otherwise, you'll hear "Fore! Fore! Fore! Fore!"

Defender

Defender is a game for three players. On hole 1, player A tries to make a score lower than that of either player B or player C. On hole 2, player B tries to score lower than players A and C and on hole 3, player C tries to get the lowest score.

This game is called defender because the players take turns defending holes throughout play. The winner is the player who successfully defends the most holes.

Eclectic
Ringer Tournament

An eclectic is a specific number of tournaments played over a designated time during a season. When an eclectic begins, all participating players shoot an 18-hole round and record their individual scores by hole (either gross or net). Players continue to play 18-hole rounds, and when a player earns a score on a hole lower than the best one previously recorded, the new lower score replaces the previous one. This process continues, and the golfer with the lowest recorded score on all holes when the tournament officially ends is the winner.

A ringer tournament is designed and scored exactly the same way as an eclectic.

Flag Tournament

In a flag tournament, each player is given a small flag prior to play. (Usually this is not a real flag but something that can easily be staked into the ground—like a tongue depressor—and is large enough for the golfer's name to be written on it.) Each participant plays her own ball as in a regular round but only until she reaches par for that 18-hole course plus the number of handicap strokes the golfer is allowed for 18 holes. At this point, the golfer plants her flag.

For example, a golfer with an 18-handicap playing a par-72 course would plant a flag wherever the ball lies after the player's 90th stroke. The player whose flag is located farthest along the course when play concludes is the winner.

Four-Ball

Four-ball is a game in which two golfers play better ball against the better ball of two other golfers, based on either gross or net scores.

Ham Shoot
Turkey Shoot

Ham shoots and turkey shoots are any-format tournaments that are held near holidays—ham shoots near Christmas or Easter and turkey shoots near Thanksgiving—with prizes that are food-related. A ham is often awarded to the winner of a ham shoot, and a turkey is often the top prize at a turkey shoot.

Horse Race

A horse race is a special tournament for a field of two-person teams playing alternate shot. The purpose of a horse race is to eliminate all but one team from the field by the end of a designated number of holes—up to 18. This is accomplished by cutting a specified number of teams at the end of each hole of play—those with the highest scores on that hole.

At the first hole, one member of each team tees off and the teams proceed with alternate shots until they hole out. The low-scoring teams continue on to the second hole and the high-scoring teams are eliminated. This process is repeated until the final hole is played for first, second, and third place, as in a horse race.

Ties for high score (to determine elimination at the end of a hole) are settled by a chip-off contested by one member from each team. This method is also used to break any low-score ties at the end of the tournament.

Irons Only

In an irons-only tournament, only iron clubs are legal—that is, woods are not permitted. Irons-only competitions can be played using different formats.

Las Vegas
Peppers

Las Vegas is a partner game in which one team member plays against a member of a rival team in a regular-style golf game. The scores that two partners make on a hole are written together. How they are written depends on whether one of the partners on a team scores par or better on the hole.

For example, on a par-4 hole, if partners on team A score a 3 and a 5 on the hole, their team score is 35. If the team B partners score a 4 and a 5 on the same par-4 hole, they have a score of 45. At the end of each hole of play, the smaller team score is subtracted from the higher team score, and the difference is the number recorded. In this example, the difference is 10 (35 subtracted from 45), so team A now has 10 "peppers"—the number of strokes they are ahead.

Now, on that same par-4 hole, if team A has scores of 5 and 6, their initial score is a 65, not a 56, because neither partner made par on the hole. If team B has scores of 4 and 5, their 45 is subtracted from team A's 65, and team B is ahead by 20 peppers.

Scores are determined in this manner for each hole of play, and the number of peppers accumulated depends on how the two teams do throughout the match. When playing Las Vegas, the most important thing to remember is how the numbers are recorded: one method is used when at least one member of a partnership makes par, and another method is used if neither of the partners scores at least par. Viva Las Vegas!

Murphy

A murphy is a wager made by one golfer to another, just before hitting onto the green, that she will be successful in getting the ball up and down on that hole.

Night Golf

Night golf is any game that is played after the sun goes down, often with lighted golf balls, holes, and tees that are provided by the golf course. Rounds of night golf are often designated as nine or fewer, because it takes much longer than usual to play in these conditions.

No Alibi

A no-alibi tournament is one in which each player's handicap becomes the number of mulligans the golfer is allowed to play during the round. A 10-handicap player would be allowed 10 mulligans, and a 30-handicap player, 30 mulligans. The person with the lowest gross score wins. The reason this is called no-alibi golf is that, with all the mulligans allowed, players have no excuse for poor scores.

One-Club Tournament

In a one-club tournament, each player must choose one club and use it for a round—putting included. Many golfers choose a 5-iron. What would your choice be?

1-2-3
3-2-1

On the first hole played in 1-2-3, the lowest score of the four players counts toward the team score; on the second hole, the two lowest of the four scores count; and on the third hole, the three lowest scores of the four count. The fourth hole goes back to the lowest one of the four counting, and so on. 3-2-1 is scored in reverse order.

Orange Ball

Much like best ball, orange ball is a game in which one of the golfers in a foursome plays with a designated ball (sometimes a colored ball is chosen to keep it visible). The team's total score is the score of the player who uses that ball plus the best score from the other three players in the group. Play with the orange ball rotates among the players hole by hole.

Par as Partner

Par as partner is a better-ball or best-ball game in which the highest score any player records on a hole is par. If someone has a score lower than par on a hole, that score is counted. And if the lowest score on any hole is higher than par, the recorded score is par.

Paradise Golf

In paradise golf, players are permitted to tee up the ball anywhere along the course, not just on the teeing ground.

Poley

A putt that is longer than the length of the flagstick—or pole—is called a poley. Some golfers have special awards for players in their group who make poleys.

Scramble
Texas (or Other State) Scramble

A scramble is a popular format that matches up teams with three or more players. All players tee off on their first hole of play, the best drive is identified, and the players in the group go to that ball's position and hit their second shot with their own ball. This format continues for the entire round of play. Each team records only one score for each hole played. The team with the lowest overall score at the end wins the competition, but both gross and net score prizes may be awarded.

A scramble may require that each team member's drive be used a certain number of times (usually three). Sometimes teams are assigned by golf course staff (or a committee) so that they are ability-balanced, with a minimum team handicap required.

In a Texas scramble, once the best shot is identified (whether it's a drive or any other shot—even a putt), the player who hit the shot is not included when the team plays from that golfer's lie.

Shamble

A shamble is a two-person team game played against other two-member teams. Each person drives off each tee, then the team decides which is the better drive. From the better drive's lie, each golfer plays his own ball into the hole. The lower of both players' scores on each hole is recorded as the team's score, and the lowest team score at the end of the round wins.

Snake (the Game)

Members of a group agree to play the game of snake at the beginning of a normal round. The player who three-putts first becomes the designated "snake" until another member of the group three-putts and thus becomes the next snake. The player who holds the title at the end of the round pays money to the other members of the group.

There are variations of this game, based on different ways of becoming the snake and different monetary penalties for losing the game.

Speed Golf
Hit-and-Run Golf

Speed golf is a game in which players try to run around the course as fast as possible during play. Another name for this game is hit-and-run golf. The player's total score for 18 holes is added to the elapsed time between the moment he drove the ball from the first tee and the moment his ball fell into the 18th hole.

Stableford
Modified Stableford

Stableford is stroke-play competition in which a player must meet or beat a fixed score on each hole in order to receive points. The player with the highest point total at the end of the competition wins.

If the fixed score is par for each hole, the player must score no more than one over par in order to receive any point(s) for play on the hole—that is, a bogey is worth 1 point for the hole, par is worth 2 points, a birdie is 3 points, an eagle is 4 points, and a double eagle is 5 points.

In amateur competitions, Stableford is typically played using handicaps.

Modified Stableford, which is played on the PGA Tour at the International Tournament, is scored as follows: -3 points for double bogey or worse, -1 point for bogey, 0 points for par, 2 points for birdie, 5 points for an eagle, and 8 for a double eagle. High score in this tournament wins.

String Tournament

In a string tournament, each player is given a length of string prior to play. The amount of string depends on what has been decided for the tournament: all players may receive equal lengths of string, or it may be apportioned by handicap—that is, 1 inch of string for each handicap stroke.

A player is permitted to move her ball a short distance—no more than the total length of the string—to improve the player's next shot. Often the string is used to move the ball a short distance from a very difficult lie—or closer to the hole before an important putt. The string can be used throughout the round of play, but each time a portion is used, it is cut off—shortening the golfer's "lifeline." The string can be used anywhere along the course and at any time, but players know they should save their string until they need it most.

The golfer with the lowest score wins the tournament, regardless of how much string she has left.

Three-Ball

Three-ball is a match-play competition in which three golfers compete against one another, each playing his own ball in regular stroke play. Each golfer is playing two distinct matches: player A is in a match with player B, and also in a match with player C; player B is in two matches, one with A and one with C; and player C is in two matches, one with A and one with B.

It's a bit like seeing the Three Musketeers out on the golf course, only it's never all for one and one for all.

Threesome (the Game)

Threesome is a match in which one person plays against the other two people (so there are two sides), with each side playing one ball so that two balls are being played by the three people. The team (or two-person) side plays alternate shots.

Umbrellas

Umbrellas is a game in which points are accumulated hole by hole as follows: 2 points for getting on the green in regulation, 2 points for the one golfer who gets closest to the hole of those who reached the green in regulation, and 2 points for making a birdie.

If one golfer wins all 6 points on a hole, his score for that hole is doubled to 12, which is called getting an umbrella. The player with the most points at the end of 18 holes is the winner.

OTHER CLUBHOUSE CONVERSATION

Ace (the Person)
Good Stick
A very good golfer is often referred to as an ace or a good stick.

Age Shooter
An age shooter is someone who shoots a score equal to or lower than his numerical age in an 18-hole round on a regulation course. For example, a golfer who is 70 years of age and shoots a score of 70 for 18 holes is an age shooter.

Course Record
The walls of many clubhouses are covered with plaques listing winners of various past tournaments played at that course. Typically, among these are plaques honoring the holders (one man and one woman) of the course record, the lowest scores ever shot on that course.

Dome Golf
Golfers are playing dome golf when they play in ideal weather under perfect course conditions. It is called dome golf because it is like playing inside an atmospherically controlled dome.

Medalist
Low Gross of the Field

The player who has the lowest gross score in a tournament is declared the medalist. This player is also referred to as having the low gross of the field.

Low Net of the Field

Sometimes a separate category is included to honor the player in a tournament with the lowest score among players using handicaps. That player is referred to as being low net of the field.

Pay Ball

In some club tournaments players are rewarded—usually with some kind of cash prize—for having the lowest score on a particular hole. This is referred to as the player earning a pay ball.

Flight
Flight Winners

A group of players put together, for award purposes, based on similar handicaps is called a flight.

There are often several flights within a tournament field. Flight winners are those who have the lowest scores among the golfers in their own flight; they may or may not have scored well enough to win the prizes for low gross or net of the field.

Ham and Egg

The term ham and egg is used informally when one of two partners plays badly on a particular hole and the other tries extra hard on the same hole in order to compensate.

After a round of play, one partner might refer to that badly played hole by saying, "We ham-and-egged it"—meaning he's grateful for the way his partner came through.

Matching Out on the Card

Sometimes ties are broken by "matching out on the card" instead of with a play-off. The players' scorecards are compared on a hole-by-hole basis, and the player with the first lower score on a hole is declared the winner.

Chip-Off

A chip-off is a method of breaking ties in which the players make sudden death chip shots, usually at the 18th hole, from a designated distance near the green. The player who hits closest to the pin wins.

Press

Two players who are competing against each other in match play often wager on who will win each hole. Once that bet is in place, if one player wins the first two holes, the other player may add a press, which is a new wager, while the original is still in place.

Anytime during subsequent holes, the player who is behind in the match can press for a new wager while all previous ones continue.

Sandbagger

Sandbagger is a derogatory term used to describe a player who wants to establish as high a handicap as possible to gain an advantage in tournaments that use handicap scoring. She plays poorly intentionally, using unnecessary strokes to raise her score and her handicap.

Sandbagger can also refer to a golfer with an honest handicap who scores unusually well in a tournament and wins. Other golfers will congratulate her and jokingly call her a sandbagger to compliment her play.

"Everything Came Together"

"Everything came together" is said of a golfer who played a round (or tournament) when all aspects of his game worked well—drives, approach shots, pitch-and-chip shots, and putts. If the golfer won the tournament, it is said that everything *really* came together.

Iceman

An iceman is someone who doesn't let anything bother him on the golf course, doesn't show emotion, takes the good with the bad, and doesn't allow pressure or distractions—like the gallery—to affect his game.

Game of Adjustments

Because golf courses are designed so differently—and even the same course can play differently depending on weather and pin placements—golf is called a game of adjustments. The player who can adapt her game to current conditions and the demands of the course will be successful.

Course Is a Good Test

A course is said to be a good test when it is set up to be fair for all levels of competition. The way the course is designed—with obstacles the golfer must negotiate, pin placements, and balance in the variety of shots a golfer needs to play—determines whether or not it is a good test. Everyone wants to play a course that is both challenging and fun.

Won 1-Up
Won 2-Up
Won 4 and 3, etc.

These terms are used to report winning scores in match play. A player who wins 1-up has won one more hole than his opponent at the end of 18 holes of play. A player who wins 2-up was two holes ahead. A player who finished "4 and 3" was four holes ahead of his opponent with three holes left to play, so the match was over.

X's on the Card

When an amateur golfer is having a bad scoring day, he may finally get so disgusted that he stops putting numbers on the scorecard and just gives himself X's instead. In order to post the round for handicap purposes, the player then uses equitable stroke control rules.

C-O-D

C-O-D is a way of choosing partners when a group of four golfers is playing with two carts. First, the two players sharing the same Cart can be partners; then the two riding in each cart can play as partners—Others; and the two Drivers of the carts can become a partnership.

Competition is played over the first six holes with one set of partners, and the middle six and the last six holes each with a change of partners. C-O-D allows everyone to be paired with everyone else through an 18-hole round.

Cross-Over

Sometimes, because of the number of people wanting to play a course at the same time, several golfers will be asked to tee off on the back nine while others tee off on the front nine. At a certain point, the two sets of golfers have to switch sides (from front nine to back and vice versa). This is called the cross-over.

Trophy Pose

When a golfer holds the finish position at the completion of the golf swing, it is called a trophy pose because it is similar to the classic designs of golfers used on etched-glass trophies and for the statues that top metal ones.

Practice Round

Prior to the official start of a tournament, those players officially entered in the tournament are allowed a practice round. This gives each player an opportunity to become familiar with the course, which is especially useful if he has not played it before.

Historic Clubs

Sometime during the 1940s, a group of golf club collectors got together and devised a system for numbering irons that would replace the old names for the clubs. The system became officially recognized worldwide and is used exclusively today. Here's a list of the old names and the corresponding numbers used today:

> The driving cleek or iron became the 1-iron.
> The mid-iron became the 2-iron.
> The mid-mashie became the 3-iron.
> The mashie iron became the 4-iron.
> The mashie became the 5-iron.
> The spade mashie became the 6-iron.
> The mashie niblick became the 7-iron.
> The niblick became both the 8- and 9-irons.

Fairway woods were also once known by name instead of number. A 2-wood was called a brassie, a 3-wood was a spoon, and a 4-wood was a baffy.

Gutta-Percha
Feathery

Gutta-percha is a hard, white substance made by evaporating the milky latex of the Malaysian tree of the same name. This substance was formed into a sphere and replaced the original golf ball, which was called a feathery, that was used in Scotland and made of a leather sphere stuffed with feathers.

Knickers

Knickers are loose-fitting pants gathered below the knee.

Plus Fours

Plus fours are sports knickers that are about four inches longer than regular knickers. They were worn and made famous by PGA Tour player Payne Stewart and earlier by Gene Sarazen.

Zamboni

Zamboni is the last name of the man who invented the machine that evens and cleans the surface of ice rinks. Once I was watching practice at a large golf facility in New Jersey and someone nearby said, "Look, they have a Zamboni," thinking that was what the golf center's range picker was called. No matter what the design or size, a range picker is always a range picker.

However, there *is* a Zamboni in golf—the grand-daughter of the inventor of the ice conditioner. She is an LPGA professional.

"Drive for Show, Putt for Dough"

Many golfers are more concerned about the way their tee shots look than how effective their short game is, so this phrase has been selected as the last one to be explained in this book. "Drive for show, putt for dough" is a gentle reminder of the importance of the short game in lowering your scores.

Whether or not you play golf, enjoy talking a great game!

Index

Index

Index

Index

JUN 0 6 2002